QUILTING
PATCHES
OF LIFE

Lori Wagner

*"Quilting Patches of Life" is dedicated to
my sister, Tina Harper.*

*We've seen a lot of "patches" in our lives
- some cheery, some dark, and some beige.*

*You were the baby left behind
as Sandy, Cheryl and I, one by one,
moved out and moved on.*

You stayed with Daddy when he needed you.

*You've opened your home and organized
almost every family gathering
– and taken photo after photo you've lovingly
shared with the photographically challenged
(and the lazy and broke).*

*You've consistently encouraged me in my
writing and speaking aspirations
and have gone above-and-beyond every time I
needed you with graphics issues for this book,
"Gates & Fences," and Affirming Faith
– even when you were crazy busy
with your own life and responsibilities.*

*You have supported me in every way.
I appreciate you as a sister,
a friend,
a giving person,
and a very talented professional.*

*Your biggest fan,
~ Lori*

CONTENTS

Acknowledgments 1

Introduction 3

Quilting Patches of Life poem 7

1. Turkey Tracks 9
    Randa Chance ~ San Antonio, TX

2. Brave Sunflower 13
    David Story ~ Pasadena, TX

3. Hole in the Barn Door 19
    Lisa Crump ~ Colorado Springs, CO

4. Hosanna 25
    Ann Kalajian ~ Manomet, MA

5. Black-Eyed Susan 31
    Lisa Riley ~ Berkley, MI

6. Garden Gate 37
    Sandra Snider ~ Minneapolis, MN

7. Broken Dishes 41
    Larry Patton ~ Troy, MI

8. Sunbonnet Sue 45
    Carolyn M. Kenney ~ Wilmington, MA

9. Honeycomb 49
    Jeanne Grief ~ Paducah, KY

10. Blind Man's Fancy 55
    Bernie Lutchman ~ Springfield, IL

11. Grandma's Fan 59
    Lori Wagner

12. Evening Star. 65
    Cristina Broomfield ~ Troy, MI

13. Rose of. Sharon. 71
    Melissa May Hoffmann ~ Rochester Hills, MI

14. Mariner's Compass 75
    Eileen Kruper ~ Troy, MI

15. East to Eden 81
    Suzanne Stoltz ~ Rolla, MO

16. Rainbow Cactus 87
    Alan Hahn ~ Waterford, MI

17. King's Highway 91
    Evans Bissonette ~ Troy, MI

18. Whirlwind. 95
    Lissa M. Lee ~ Madisonville, LA

19. Flower Basket 101
    Patty Cayten ~ Niles, OH

20. Joy Bells 105
    Irvin L. Rozier ~ Blackshear, GA

21. Capital T 111
    John Wood ~ Las Vegas, NV

22. Crown of Thorns 115
    Rachel Lowrence ~ Southfield, MI

23. Garden Walk. 119
    Margie Stoller ~ Bloomfield Hills, MI

24. Britches 125
Brad Paulson ~ Spokane, WA

25. Dove in the Window 129
Dixie Phillips ~ Floyd, IA

26. Anvil 133
Karrie Vandewater ~ Stuttgart, Germany

27. Follow the Leader 139
Julianne Jones ~ Wanganui, New Zealand

28. Pinwheel 145
Sharon K. Wilson ~ Clarkston, MI

29. Hens and Chicks 149
Florence Koski ~ Covington, KY

30. Dancing Bear 155
Steve Lockman ~ Lancaster, MN

31. Treasure Chest 159
Jan Ross ~ Willard, OH

32. Job's Tears 165
Brad Erlandson ~ Clarkston, MI

33. Beggar's Block 171
Karen Elengikal ~ Sydney, Australia

34. Cathedral Window 175
Christine Gibson ~ Rochester Hills, MI

35. The Kitchen Woodbox 181
Jane Doe ~ Anytown, USA

36. Arkansas Traveler 185
Paul Phillips ~ Floyd, IA

37. Pig's Tail 191
   Maria Taormina ~ Grand Blanc, MI

38. Buzzard's Roost 197
   Julie Arduini ~ Youngstown, OH

39. Lone Star 201
   Carolyn McKenzie ~ Auburn Hills, MI

40. Hopes and Wishes 205
   Lori Wagner

41. The Backing 211
   Lori Wagner

42. The Common Thread 215
   Lori Wagner

Bios
Affirming Faith Writing Contest Winners.................218
FaithWriters 220
Friends and Family 222

Notes 225
Contact Information................................... 226

ACKNOWLEDGMENTS

A great big THANK YOU to everyone who shared their stories for this project. All contributors offered willingly, without compensation, and their stories have touched my life.

Thank you, my wonderful family, for all your love and support, and my church family at Faith Apostolic Church of Troy and Pastor and Mrs. Marvin Walker. I appreciate every one of you so much.

Good people of the Barnes & Noble Writer's Connection, thank you for being my sounding board and helping me develop my writing skills – and for your patience all the times I talked too much.

Thank You, Jesus, for entrusting me with this project that has affected so many people even before its publication. Thank You for Your sweet presence in my office as I edited and worked on each chapter – and our rendezvous in the kitchen.

INTRODUCTION

I swept the dusty wood floor that morning, not really thinking about one thing or the other. The kids were safely off to school, and I was enjoying the quiet as I putzed in my kitchen. My first book, *Gates & Fences* was back from the printer and doing well. Although I had dabbled with thoughts of writing a follow-up book, my main work focus was on marketing and promoting *Gates & Fences* – not beginning another full-length project. But as I guided the broom back and forth, my thoughts meandering here and there, the Lord dropped something in my spirit I could not ignore. He called it *Quilting Patches of Life*.

I saw the individual days and experiences of human existence pieced by the Lord into a lovely creation – a unique, functional work of warmth, beauty and purpose – a quilt of life. The different aspects of quilting unfolded into revelatory spiritual truths, and I started to cry, broom in hand, marveling that God would even bother speaking to me.

Rather than stand there babbling, I wiped my eyes, sat down at my laptop, and thought through the many steps of the quilting process.

After much planning, collecting and cutting, the pieces of the top are sewn together. I likened our days and seasons to pieces of patchwork in all different sizes, shapes, colors and patterns.

In our dark days God gives us hope and speaks precious things into our broken lives. The blessings of happy days I saw as pink floral patches that provide the lessons we learn on the mountain tops about God's goodness and provision. Even the boring days, what I thought of as "strips of beige," are part of our lives for a reason. God exhorts and encourages His people in the mundane things of life . . . like sweeping a kitchen floor. Yes, God speaks to us throughout our lives, and sometimes we even listen.

The theme poem, *Quilting Patches of Life,* slipped from my heart to my fingers to the page. Then I began researching different quilt patterns and writing chapters, inviting some of my friends to contribute their stories. I felt compelled to open the project for wider input, so Affirming Faith conducted its first writing contest. Via the internet, writers forums and news media, Christians of all denominations were invited to send in their stories.

As you read, you will find different expressions of individual faith. Our doctrines may be different, but we all look to Jesus for our strength, guidance, peace and hope. He speaks to us as we seek Him, no matter where we are in our spiritual journeys. We can learn from each other, and we can all grow to be more in God.

To bring continuity to the project, each person's story was titled with the name of a quilt pattern. Each chapter begins with the writer's personal account, then I add my thoughts to what he/she shared.

It is my prayer that readers of *Quilting Patches of Life* will be encouraged and inspired by its true stories. Grab a box of tissue and turn the page as we explore the many ways God speaks to His people today.

~ Lori Wagner

Quilting Patches of Life
Lori Wagner

Patches of florals
Checkers and stripes
Ginghams and plaids
Cheery and bright

The poke of the needle
With each rise and dip
Sharp blades of the scissors
With each snip and clip

Fashioned in trapezoids
Circles and squares
Cut with precision
Assembled with care

Hand sewn with a purpose
Patterns and groups
Create counterpane
Then rest in the hoop

Gray, beige and black
Strips dull and bland
Placed in a pattern
By God's sovereign hand

On the lap of the Master
Batted and backed
He binds it together
To place on His rack

Seasons of sunshine
And blushing bouquets
The laughter of children
Warm holidays

Unique in appearance
A keepsake and treasure
With function and beauty
Made for His pleasure

Contrasted by storm clouds
Trials and need
The mundane, everyday
Lives that we lead

Whether mountains or valleys
Or treadmills unending
A pattern of days
God's crafting, or mending

Bits of bright joy
Dark segments of strife
The routine of existence
Patches of life

His purpose in focus
Our hearts safely rest
Believing, trusting
The Quilter knows best

*Quilts are like poetry
in fabric.*

Turkey Tracks
Submitted by Randa Chance of San Antonio, Texas

I woke up in a fog. I was exhausted beyond description. My alarm clock had been ringing for an hour, and I slept right through it. As per normal, my family had come home late the night before from church where my husband serves as the assistant pastor. It was one of those weeks. We had spent no quality time together – not even one night, and I had not slept well because my mind was whirling with tasks needing to be completed – church situations, family issues, and just weird random things. You know how it is when you can't sleep.

I launched my body out of bed, glared at the alarm clock, and freaked out. I had TEN (count 'em) 10 minutes to get ready for work, dress the kids, comb my daughter's hair, and get out the door. My eyes were bloodshot and swollen from lack of sleep, and my breath – well, it could have knocked over a water buffalo. Deodorant was not even in my thought process as I scrambled for my clothes and threw my hair into a ponytail.

I shook Devon awake, marched her into the bathroom, combed her hair and yanked her clothes over her head. As we do every morning, I prayed with her quickly and gave her a hug and kiss. She was very quiet through the entire progression of events. Finally, as I was getting ready to rush out the door, a tiny voice stopped me in my tracks.

"Mama, can I hold you for just a minute before you leave?"

I rolled my eyes (not where she could see, of course), sighed inwardly, and glanced at the clock. *Two more minutes won't make that much difference,* I thought, so I sat down on the edge of the bed. She crawled into my lap and curled her skinny little body into the perfect size for holding. Resting her head on my chest, she let out a sigh. I rocked her for a moment and patted her back as frantic thoughts of traffic, bills, and then, "Dear God, I forgot to brush my teeth!" ran through my head.

She looked up at me and said "Mama, um . . ."

"What is it, baby?"

"Oh, never mind."

"No, please tell me," I said, "You know you can tell me anything. What is it?" I thought maybe she had been hurt or was upset.

Her blue eyes shined up at me, and in a very serious voice she said, "Well, Mama, well, it's just that . . . you – you mean so much to me."

My chaotic thoughts came to a standstill, and I melted into a puddle. I looked up at the crown molding edging the ceiling and tried not to cry as tears prickled the backs of my eyes.

"You just gave me the nicest gift I've ever received," I told her. I held her close and kissed the top of her five-year-old head. She clung to me, not wanting to let go.

When I finally left for work, Devon was standing at the top of the stairs, all smiles, and this time she didn't hesitate to speak her mind.

"I love you with all my heart, Mama!" she yelled. She ran to my bedroom window and stood on a chair to wave at me as I drove out of sight.

If I had just brushed by her request to hold her, and instead rushed off to work without a backward glance, I would have missed one of the most precious treasures a mom can receive. Too many times I have stepped into my "Superwoman-full-steam-ahead" mode and zoomed out the door with my jet pack, neglecting to notice the tiny little people placed in my care. But thank God I stopped that day to hold my daughter. It made all the difference in the world to me.

❃

Oh, Randa, how I relate to your story. If I left prints behind, the ground around me would look like the bottom of a poultry coop – tracks running here, scratchings over there. Sometimes I feel like a turkey scrabbling and pecking as the dear Lord whispers, "Be still, Lori" – or my children plop on the couch next to my desk waiting to see my face instead of the back of my head while I work on my current "I just have to finish this . . ." project.

The quilt pattern known today as *Turkey Tracks* has an interesting history. It started out as the *Tents of Kedar*, a design created in black and white depicting the dwellings of the nomadic tribes of the Old Testament. At the time of it's writing, the Scripture reading to "dwell in the tents of Kedar" meant to be cut off from worship of the true God.

Over time, the quilt pattern received a new name, *Wandering Foot*. A legend surrounded this pattern that a young man sleeping under a *Wandering Foot* quilt would never settle down and have a family. The pattern, due to the supposed curse, received its third name, *Turkey Tracks*, which I chose to title this chapter.

It is easy for life's busyness to consume our days. We may find ourselves living in "condos of Kedar" or rushing around in "cars of Kedar," cut off from what's really important. Ishmael's descendants wandered the desert in nomadic tents, but God's chosen people were established in the Promised Land – rooted and grounded in God as long as they remained faithful to their covenant with Him.

Randa's story encourages me to stop the squawking, flapping and scratching of life and take time for the things that matter most: our relationships with our loved ones and with the Lord.

How much piecin' a quilt is like livin' a life.
You can give the same kind of pieces to two persons,
and one will make a "nine patch,"
and one'll make a "wild goose chase,"
and there will be two quilts made of the same kind of pieces, and
jest as different as they can be.
And that is jest the way with livin'.
The Lord sends us the pieces,
but we cut them out and put 'em together . . .
and there's a heap more in the cuttin' out and the sewin'
than there is in the caliker.

~ Eliza Calvert Hall in "Aunt Jane of Kentucky"

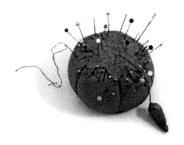

~ 2 ~
Brave Sunflower
Submitted by David Story of Pasadena, Texas

I knew her name a month before I met her. When I started my job at the Christian bookstore everyone talked about Penny. "Oh, you'll like Penny," I heard over and over.

The following month, Penny returned to work, and I had to agree with my coworkers. She was a special lady. I was surprised to learn that what I thought had been a resort-type vacation turned out to be a trip to see her husband who worked in Iraq – a location not making my top ten list of vacation spots given the fighting and instability in the region.

I later learned that Penny's son was killed in Afghanistan. Waiting at a landing zone after completing a mission that included taking food to Afghani civilians, Phillip's battalion engaged in a battle that took his life.

Penny told me the story – how she answered the door to her apartment and received the news of her son's death. She told me how the company her husband worked for flew him from Iraq to Afghanistan, where the body was, so he could return home with his son.

On a rainy Sunday morning, my family and I drove to church. Not our church – Penny's. As we made the turn into the parking lot, my wife Lynette looked over and asked, "You going to be a gentleman and let us out at the front of the church?"

I laughed and was about to say yes when the church came into view. This was our first visit, and I didn't quite know what to expect, but the scene in front of me wasn't it.

13

My daughter Amy spoke first. "Who are they?"

"I'm not sure," I said.

The three of us stared wide-eyed at row after row of motorcycles in the church parking lot.

"Are you sure we've got the right church?" Lynette asked.

I looked at the sign in front of the building. "Yeah, that's the one." And then I remembered. "You know, now that I think about it, Penny did say something about a motorcycle group . . . the, uh . . . the Patriot Guard."

We pulled into the parking lot and made our way to the front of the church. The loose gravel and potholes made for a bumpy crossing – especially in the old clunker I drove, but we made it. As soon as I pulled up to the drop-off, a man in a military uniform walked to the passenger's side and, umbrella in hand, assisted Lynette and Amy out of the car.

By the time I parked and made it inside the church, the foyer was packed with an eclectic combination of people in military uniforms, motorcycle "gang" attire, and Sunday-go-to-Meetin' clothes. I found Lynette and Amy, and we made our way into the sanctuary to one of the pews about halfway down the aisle. Penny saw us immediately.

"So glad you could come," she said, then introduced us to some of her church family. She caught her husband's attention and motioned for him to come over. Carson greeted us with a tired smile and a handshake, then they moved on to greet other guests and friends.

Alone again, we settled in and looked around. Two men were at the front of the church setting up a professional looking video camera. "Must be the people from the news station," I said.

Suddenly, a man with a smaller camera walked in front of us and took our picture. He shrugged and said, "They gave me the camera and told me to start taking pictures." We laughed, and he walked away.

The sanctuary filled and all the chattering ceased as the praise and worship team entered and the service began – a service celebrating God, family, and country. In between songs we watched video clips that documented the faith of our country's founding fathers; how their strong religious convictions laid the groundwork for our great nation. The pastor spoke of service: service to others, service to country, and service to God.

The message concluded with the minister and worship team singing a wonderful rendition of *"How Great Thou Art"* ending with the repeated words "How great You are." I looked down the aisle at Amy and saw tears in her eyes. They would be the first of many.

After the singing, a slide show began. Images of people serving flashed before our eyes: church members building and cleaning the church, Sunday school classes filled with children and adults.

Suddenly the images changed to photos from 9/11. Two burning towers. The smoldering Pentagon. Men and women rescuing the fallen.

Earlier in the week, Penny told me her husband put together the slide show. I looked over as she and Carson watched the presentation and saw Carson wipe tears from his eyes.

Following the 9/11 shots, a picture of a grave marker consumed the screen. It read:

Phillip C. George
U.S. Marines
KIA - Afghanistan
Born - 9.3.82
Died - 8.18.05
"His Grace Is Sufficient"

The photo faded, and an image of Phillip dressed in his formal military uniform took its place. The whole church went silent as the image remained on the screen. The realization hit me that this young man was not only Penny and Carson's son, but also the son of this congregation of believers. The tear-streaked faces in the sanctuary evidenced their admiration for their fallen soldier.

The Pastor regained composure long enough to pray for the fallen and for those who had served down through the ages. Then he introduced a special speaker.

A woman from *Home of the Brave*, a group of ladies from Vidor, Texas, took the stage and microphone and explained why she and her friends had come to make this presentation to Penny and another woman named Zaida Walters. She gave a brief history of memory quilts and told of their tradition dating back to the Civil War.

"Every quilt is unique," she said. "Each has a patch with the name of the fallen soldier, another patch with the name of a soldier killed during the Vietnam War, and one replica patch from the Civil War."

Penny, Carson and Mrs. Walters were called to the front of the church. With tears in their eyes, women from *Home of the Brave* made their presentation. We all smiled, lumps in our throats, as the quilts were unfolded and held high for all to see.

I was moved beyond words, watching with tears as Penny received her quilt. A quilt made by some very special women. A quilt made in honor of her son, Phillip. A quilt made with love and care in a tradition passed from generation to generation, conflict to conflict, since the Civil War.

As I watched Penny accept the quilt, my thoughts drifted back to some of the things I'd seen in the last year working together. Once a customer came in to purchase a Bible for a soldier about to go off to battle. Penny was there to talk to her and encourage her. I watched in amazement as she, one who lost her own son in war kept that experience to herself and instead smiled, nodded, listened and promised to support this woman and her son in prayer.

Then there were the customers who suffered losses. The ones who came in to find something – a book or some inspirational item – anything that would encourage them through their trials. And, as always, Penny was there. First she listened to their stories, then she shared her own.

There was one customer I will never forget. Penny and I were at the register when a lady came in and looked straight at her.

"I want to thank you for saving my life," she said. "I was contemplating suicide the last time I came into this store. You prayed for me that day."

The tears started, and Penny left the counter to talk to her. I don't know how the rest of the conversation went, but there was Penny again, ministering to someone in need. And this time around, she caught a glimpse of the harvest.

I asked Penny what she was going to do with her memory quilt. She told me she had a place picked out on a wall at home. She plans to hang it and let it serve as a reminder of the sacrifices life requires and good people offer – like a kind group of women from Vidor, Texas, who honor fallen soldiers with tangible expressions of compassion – like a courageous young man who believed he was doing what God called him to do and paid the ultimate price – and in my estimation, like a brave soldier of the cross, my friend Penny, who reaches beyond her own heartache to minister God's healing and comfort to others. Thank you, Penny.

Soldier Boy, Freedom Quilt, Glory, Hero's Crown – all would have been appropriate names for LCpl Phillip George's story. But as I prayed about the title selection for this chapter, I realized this is Penny's story. Through David's sharing of his friend and coworker, this literary introduction to Penny created a picture in my mind of a courageous, cheerful and giving woman – a *Brave Sunflower.*

Sunflower plants, in the bud stage, rotate on their stems. They begin each day facing east, then track the sun as it travels west, eventually returning to an eastward orientation. However, once sunflowers bloom, their stems become stiff and freeze the flower facing east . . . always awaiting the coming sunrise.

When a sunflower has fully matured, it provides food and oil used in cooking and soaps – giving itself for nourishment and fuel. Besides their many useful functions, cheerful sunflowers simply brighten our days with radiant blooms – like Penny's cheerful disposition and kind nature.

A mature sunflower stands its ground, even when the sun no longer shines on its face. In our times of darkness, we can stand tall, knowing we will see the light again – as sure as the morning sun.

~ 3 ~
Hole in the Barn Door
Submitted by Lisa Crump of Colorado Springs, Colorado

Lazy Lis. That's what Mr. Bigham, my P.E. teacher, called me in elementary school. He said it in jest because I was so active, but it stuck just the same. *Lively Lis* would have been a more accurate nickname. I wanted to do so many things, and I wanted to excel in them all. My desire to learn gymnastics kept me on a diligent practice schedule. I strove for perfection, working every day during gym, after school, and at home. I loved being active and also rode horses and competed in equestrian events.

When I reached Junior High, I became nervous about the heightened academic requirements. Realizing school was going to be more difficult, I reluctantly gave up gymnastics to devote more time to my education. It was a tough decision, but I was able to let gymnastics go and threw myself into my studies. I couldn't give up my time with the horses, though. My love for riding kept me in the saddle.

Throughout my elementary years, I had a voracious appetite. I consumed large quantities of food yet stayed slim and healthy. At any given meal I ate as much as my father who had the physically demanding jobs of farming and ranching. However, as my activity level decreased and my eating habits stayed the same, I began to put on extra weight. People noticed, and I was embarrassed.

I hated the way I felt, so I began starving myself and was soon thoroughly immersed in anorexia. For nine months of the seventh grade I was extremely hungry, irritable and weak. My misery compelled me to begin eating again. So I ate . . . and kept on eating, developing poor dietary habits throughout my high school years.

Despondent about my weight, in my freshman year of college I attempted to win the battle of the bulge with a new method that allowed me to eat all I wanted. I began binging on food and then purging it from my system by self-induced vomiting. This satisfied my appetite for food, but kept my body from storing unwanted calories.

The bulimic binging and purging continued in secret throughout my college years, my marriage and even into motherhood. In varying degrees, for 13 years I used this method to maintain my weight. On the outside everything appeared great. Internally, I was destroying my body. But more than that, with every binge and purge I lost more than food. My personal dignity and feelings of spiritual worth were retched from my heart and soul.

I had committed my life to God when I was ten years old. I attended a Christian college and was actively involved in church all the years I suffered with this terrible eating disorder. Yet I kept this part of my life separated from God – or so I thought. The Lord loved me so much He did not allow me to remain comfortable behind the facade.

God began to put me in circumstances that hindered my secret habit until one day revelation dawned. A counselor at a church camp, I was teaching junior and senior high girls about giving their all to Jesus when it hit me. I looked around at the faces of the girls looking to me for their example and was struck with the realization that I had fallen into my debilitating trap at their age. I began to see what a hypocrite I was; trying to instruct the girls in the Lord when I had not surrendered my whole life to Him. A new longing awakened within me – life must be about more than this oppressive habit. I wondered if I might even die from this addictive hidden sin, shocking my husband and leaving my beautiful young daughter behind – and all for what? If I did die, what impact would my life leave on those around me when my covert behavior was exposed?

Through godly conviction, the Lord began to make His Word come alive in my struggle. "Do not grieve the Holy Spirit of God" (Ephesians 4:30a) pierced me. Scripture echoed in my head. "Your body is a temple of the Holy Spirit, who is in you . . . honor God with your body." (1 Corinthians 6:19-20 NIV) I understood that a holy God would not desire to live in a self-abused temple, and I wanted to please the Lord above all else.

After the reproof, the Lord provided again through His Word the encouragement and strength I needed to begin spiritual and physical transformation. Psalm 46:10a became one of my life verses, "Be still and know that I am God." This passage helped me refocus on who God is: all powerful and all knowing in every difficult moment. Another verse met me right where I was: "For God did not give us a spirit of timidity, but a spirit of power, of love and of self-discipline." (2 Timothy 1:7 NIV) The Lord used His Word to motivate me with His love, empower me to grow, and develop the self-discipline I needed to change my life.

Hindered by pride and shame, it took some time before I experienced full deliverance. I had been a slave physically, emotionally, and spiritually to my addiction and desire to appear in control. Later I learned that my perfectionist tendencies were compulsive behaviors that needed to be addressed. Spiritual counseling or the assistance of such resources as Remuda Ranch, a residential treatment facility for people suffering with eating disorders, could have helped me through the process had I turned to them.

Although I struggled in silence, I was not alone. God did not leave me or forsake me. He led me to begin journaling about my experiences. This established a private but powerful method of accountability between God and me. With each entry I bared my innermost being before the Lord. I wrote of my weaknesses and dependence on God, and also of how the Lord strengthened and helped me. As I progressed, there were still many times I felt I would never be totally free of the bondage. I longed for the life I felt was on the other side.

21

The Lord has brought healing into my land. The Word says in Habbakuk 3:19 that God gives us the ability to overcome our own unique struggles, and I praise God that He has for me. Now I try to help others as God has enabled me to boldly "proclaim freedom for the captives." (Isaiah 61:1b NIV)

I am free now to share the hidden torments of my compulsive disorder. For me it was eating, for someone else it could be shopping, cleaning, working or any number of other things. In my life, admitting the secret and opening my heart to self examination and the light of the Word silenced the voice of my enemy. I am liberated and whole because of Jesus.

I have learned that I do not have to be or appear perfect – for myself, for others or for God. The perfection I was desperately searching for was found when I acknowledged my weakness and found strength to overcome in God. I will never be perfect, but I am complete as I live my life surrendered to a perfect God. Now, well into the second half of life, I am consumed by a desire to finish well for my Lord. Never before have I felt so alive in Christ; aligned with His purposes!

�֍

Lisa grew up in a Christian home. She gave her heart to Jesus at an early age and had a committed walk with God, but there was something holding her back. Her secret struggle with perfectionism manifested in eating disorders that tapped her spiritually and physically.

Her struggle brought to mind the quilt pattern *Hole in the Barn Door*. The most structurally sound barn would be compromised by a hole in the door. Critters, cold and precipitation would have access into the barn; livestock, warmth and provisions could escape.

Lisa had her spiritual "barn." She knew the Lord and served Him, yet she had a "hole" in the door, an opening that prevented her from being all she could be for the Lord she loved. Things were creeping in and seeping out that undermined her ability to serve God with all her heart.

Strapped in condemnation's restraint, many of God's children lack the freedom and strength to be all they can in Christ. But there is hope. Our "holes" can be plugged with the help of the Holy Spirit. Just as Lisa learned to overcome in her private battleground, the Lord will give every believer the grace and strength they need for abundant, victorious living when they turn to Him and trust in His Word.

*Love is the thread
that binds.*

~ 4 ~
Hosanna
Submitted by Ann Kalajian of Manomet, Massachusetts

The summer of 1947 Hripsimeh and I, nervous and afraid, prepared to board the plane that would carry us to our new home. Little more than girls, we stepped across the threshold leaving behind our loved ones for a new life in a strange place – with men we had never met.

Our parents arranged our marriages. Daddy, a clerk in the Armenian Orthodox church, was an official in our community. Mom had her own business creating fine linens and beautiful needlework. She also had cancer. As the disease took its toll on her body, her last wish was to see her remaining single daughters married. It was that wish that propelled us forward on this unnerving journey.

Daddy had borrowed money to cover our travel expenses from Damascus to Boston, and now we were on our way. We took our seats and searched through the window for the familiar faces of those who came to see us off. Our eyes held fast to Mothers' as our plane pulled away from the terminal, knowing we would never see her again in this world.

The long flight took us to Istanbul where we had reservations to lodge overnight. We checked in to our hotel, exhausted physically and emotionally, and headed towards our room.

Suddenly, two men approached, taking us by surprise in the hotel lobby.

"Would you ladies like to see the city?" asked one of the brash young Turks with a provocative smile.

Our mother's admonition to be safe was scarcely needed to protect us from the danger lurking in the invitation. Fear alone was enough. I attempted to hide the chill racing up and down my spine and thanked the man, politely declining his offer. Hripsimeh and I turned and hurried down the corridor to our room glancing over our shoulders to make sure the men didn't follow.

The hotel was lovely with a fine restaurant, and although hunger gnawed at our bellies, we refused to venture beyond our locked door. Instead we nibbled seeds like frightened mice and spent a restless night in our room. Morning came – finally – and we left the hotel for our Pan Am flight to America.

We arrived in New York, disembarked from the plane and scanned the crowd for the faces on the photos we received before we left Syria. Dismayed, we realized no one was there to meet us. We were stranded in New York City. We spoke to the people around us, and the panic at finding ourselves alone heightened as no one understood our words. Fluent in Arabic and Armenian, we attempted to communicate in both languages receiving only vacant stares and apologetic shrugs in return.

One shock followed another as I locked eyes with an imposing African American man walking straight for me. Never having seen a black man before, my eyeballs grew steadily larger with each of his long strides until the very tall, very dark man stood directly in front of me, still probing me with his gaze.

"Where are you going?" he asked in French.

My fear subsided at his words. "Our fiances are in Boston, but they aren't here to meet us," I answered. I knew only a little of the language, but it was enough to communicate.

"Do you know anyone in New York?" he asked.

I pulled a piece of paper from my purse and replied, "Our aunt's sister-in-law owns a shoe shop in the city. She isn't expecting us, but here's her name and address."

The benevolent stranger called a taxi, and before we knew it we pulled in the drive to the lady's house. Taken by complete surprise, the distant relative greeted us warmly. After hearing our story, she placed a call to Boston to solve the mystery of why no one was in New York to meet us. She spoke to our fiances' father and learned they had not received the telegraph our father sent. No one came because no one knew we were there.

With that revelation, my sister and I settled in for the night, until, that is, the brothers arrived from Boston at 1:00 a.m. Anxious to get a glimpse of them, we peeked through the French doors of our room as the young men entered the house.

My heart sank.

A familiar concern assaulted my senses with a new urgency – the same feeling that began haunting me when I first saw my fiance's photo back home. Hripsimeh seemed happy with her George, but I could not bring myself to accept that I would marry this man – that I would spend my life with someone that stirred this apprehension within me. Although I said nothing, my heart was screaming *No!*

Morning dawned, and at last we came face to face. I struggled between my impulse to run and the desire to follow my mother's wishes, ultimately resolving to give my betrothed a fair chance. After all, I didn't really know him.

Our foursome traveled to Boston where my sister and I stayed with our fiances' family. They were more than just in-laws-to-be, but also our relatives, the sons of our mother's nephew. We spent time together. I even allowed myself to be hugged and kissed, but I felt nothing. The young man was an artist and attempted to show me his portfolio, but I wasn't interested in looking at it.

I began to get ill. My leg became inflamed and I could barely walk the pain was so great. A doctor called to the house diagnosed my condition as a bad case of nerves and prescribed a treatment of antibiotics.

Knowing my condition was due to stress, my future mother-in-law took matters into her hands and called a relative for advice – another uncle who lived in the area. "I'll cut off my arm if she marries my son," she told him. She knew my secret.

This second uncle's family came to the house we were staying at and took everyone out on a Sunday afternoon excursion. We had ice cream then visited his home, a beautiful mansion.

During a tour of the house, my cousin whisked me away to the attic on the pretense of wanting to show me something.

He spoke in Turkish saying, "Osanna, this is America. Do you like this boy?" I didn't want to cry, but the floodgate burst, and my tears would not be stopped. "Don't go home," he continued. "I'll send you to school. You won't have to get married. I'll talk to my dad and he'll get you out of the house." For the first time in a long time, my heart felt a measure peace.

All the relatives had a meeting, and it was decided Hripsimeh and I would leave the house we were staying at and move in with this second uncle. George came each day to see my sister, and I had three months to marry, begin college, or return to Syria.

Sometimes what seems to be an accident – even a disappointment – turns out to be a blessing. In all the activity, Hripsimeh and I left our robes in Damascus. Never expecting to see them again, Mother's act of thoughtfulness spanned the globe, bringing with it our robes and the answer to my dilemma.

The doorbell of my uncle's home announced a visitor. Since none of the immediate family was around to answer it, I opened the door to receive a lady and her two daughters. They stood in the entry way bearing a package for me and Hripsimeh – our forgotten robes sent by our Mother with a friend.

After a visit and our thanks, the lady returned to her home in Watertown, a city known for its dense Armenian population. She immediately called on her next-door-neighbor whose son was an eligible bachelor.

"You'll like her, Charlie," she said. "She has long hair and a trim figure. She'll be going back soon. You should meet her." Charlie's mom called my aunt the same day asking if the family could visit. When they arrived, another tour of the house began leaving me and Charlie alone in the living room. We talked for ten minutes, and I knew right away. I liked him. I told my aunt, "If he calls, I'll go with him." She was surprised and asked, "How can you tell he's nice?" I just could.

At 9:00 a.m. the next day, the phone rang. It was Charlie, and it was his day off work.

"Would you like to spend the day together?" he asked.

Of course, I said, "Yes."

He took me to a beautiful park with a stream running through it. I admit, I have a nervous nature. When Charlie wanted to take me on a canoe ride, and the boat rocked as I stepped in, I was terrified. I tried to relax, but he could tell I was uncomfortable and brought me back to shore.

We spent the entire day together, including dinner at an exclusive restaurant. A waiter carried a lobster by, and I was afraid to order anything. I'd never seen such a creature, much less want to eat something like that. Again, Charlie understood. He ordered a chicken dinner for me that I was too shaky and nervous to eat. But he didn't seem to mind.

Each day after work Charlie came with gifts for me and my aunt. He brought flowers, fruit, candy and ice cream every day for three weeks. When we were alone, I could tell he wanted to kiss me. He was too shy, so I leaned over and kissed him. The next day he was still shy, but he worked up the courage to say, "Osanna, I'm interested in you. What do I have to do?"

I told him about all the expenses – the bills, plane ticket and paperwork. "I'll speak to your uncle and take care of everything," he said. "Let's go buy a ring."

I started to cry, and this time my tears were for joy. We drove to the jeweler, who paraded sparkling rings before us in all sizes and shapes. Charlie chose a beautiful blue diamond, and we began planning our wedding. A generous and kind man, he paid for all my expenses and much of my sister's as well.

Only two weeks remained before I had to leave the country. Because I did not know what to say, I had not written my family. Now, with much to say, I sent off a five-page letter including Charlie's photo and the money for my travel expenses so Daddy could repay the loan for our tickets.

I was nineteen years old, and Hripsimeh fifteen. We were young and didn't know what the future held for us as we left our family and home. But one thing I did know – God was with me. I learned this lesson early in life, and it was confirmed one unforgettable evening when I was still a young girl.

From a young age I prayed faithfully every night before I went to sleep. One evening as I knelt beside my bed to pray, I saw something dark slithering down the wall in the blackness. I screamed, and my parents came running to discover a poisonous snake descending on my bed. It would have landed right on top of me if I had climbed into bed without praying. Daddy killed it and I was safe.

"Because you were praying, you were saved from the snake," Mom said, and I believe what she said was true. Throughout my life God has saved me from many dangers: the men in Istanbul, arriving in New York alone and not knowing the language, bringing understanding people into my life that helped me along the way and being rescued from a marriage to someone I didn't care for. God always made a way for me – providing for me and protecting me.

❀

The name Osanna is Armenian for Hosanna, which is interpreted "save now" according to Psalm 118:25. When she married Charles Kalajian , Osanna changed her name to the more Americanized Ann, but the name imparted by her parents at her birth on Palm Sunday still waves as a banner over her life – a banner that says, "God saves and provides."

The quilt pattern *Hosanna* is also called *The Palm*. In Jewish tradition, the palm branch is a symbol of triumph and victory, as well as the prosperity of the righteous. Our understanding of it today is as a symbol of God's salvation and also a New Testament expression of praise and adoration to the One who saves.

Just as Jesus made His triumphant entry into Jerusalem on what we now call Palm Sunday, He's still entering hearts and lives today . . . coming with salvation, and provision . . . and still worthy of our praise and adoration.

Black-Eyed Susan
Submitted by Lisa Riley of Berkley, Michigan

I was sixteen years old, a junior in high school and pregnant.

"John's 21 and a foreman at his work," I told my parents during a tension-filled family meeting. Knowing it wasn't the ideal situation, I spilled out my love-enhanced list of John's finer qualities certain Mom and Dad would be happy for me once they saw what a catch I'd made. "He drives a Cadillac and lives in Birmingham," I continued.

The words were true when I spoke them; however, soon things began to change. Losing his job was the first blow. Next a tow truck hauled off the old white Cadillac. Although I had been truthful when I told my parents John lived in affluent Birmingham, I skipped over the fact that he lived with his family in a less than well-to-do section of the city.

Having a baby on the way can alter a person's perspective on reality. With high hopes for the future, I disregarded the current unfavorable circumstances and married John anyway. I was six months along with a white dress draped over a huge mound of baby belly as we exchanged vows at a simple home ceremony in May. It wasn't a fairy tale wedding, but I was happy – a married woman in love and overjoyed with the expectation of my first child soon to arrive.

Continuing in non-fairy-tale fashion, my "happily ever after" dreams began spiraling downward immediately after the ceremony. During the reception John drank so much we were unable to go on our honeymoon. I was disappointed, but I tried to look on the bright side. *It's just one night, and we have the rest of our lives together,* I thought as we drove back to the house with John's family.

The architecture of the Birmingham house was unusual. In most homes, the walls connect to the ceiling, but at John's house a four-inch gap opened along the top of every interior wall. We could hear everything said and done in the room next to ours. My wedding night was less than romantic as I lay next to my inebriated husband saying good night to everyone in the house like a scene from *The Waltons.* "Goodnight, Dad. Goodnight, Rick."

Resilient and determined, I resumed my high school classes waddling up and down the hallways with my 60 pound weight gain. In June I finished the 11th grade. In July I celebrated my 17th birthday. In August I delivered a beautiful baby girl. My precious Shannon weighed in at 9 pounds 4 ounces. She was a content baby, and I loved being her mommy.

John and I continued to live with his family after Shannon's birth. The physical abuse began slowly – maybe with a kick out of bed or a shove across the room. I felt bad for John. He was only mimicking what he learned growing up watching his father abuse his mother. I thought I would be able to "fix it." With everything in me I wanted to make this marriage work. And despite his faults, John was a good father and bonded closely with our baby girl.

We eventually moved our little family into our own home. It was something I had been looking forward to, but again my hopes were dashed. With no family around to intervene, the fights and physical abuse grew worse.

John went into business for himself cutting down trees. Work was sporadic, and when he did complete a job he drank heavily, often sleeping through the alarm the next day. One morning, concerned that he would lose his business, I prodded him to wake up. He was miserably hung over and didn't want to get out of bed. That's when he began punching me.

Still in our first year of marriage, John started talking about divorce. "I thought marrying you would change me, but it didn't,"

32

he said admitting he wanted to party with his friends more than he wanted to be married to me.

"Please just give us a chance," I begged.

We stayed together, and the fighting escalated. I broke my toe trying to defend myself as John shoved me down the stairs, picked me up by the hair on each side of my head and shook me into the wall. I filed a complaint with the police, but I didn't follow through and nothing became of it.

The abuse progressively worsened. I was too frightened to call the police again. John would be jailed for a second offence, and I was terrified when I considered what he would do to me after he got out.

Thoughts of suicide taunted me with a way of escape. It wasn't that I wanted to die, but the thought of killing myself gave me a twisted sense of power. At least I would be in control of that final decision: I could take my own life before John killed me.

Desperate and afraid, I began to pray. I cried out to the Lord begging, "God, please make Yourself real to me." And He did. Through a lady He brought me in contact with, I came to know Jesus as my Savior, repenting of my sins, being baptized in His precious Name and receiving the beautiful gift of His Spirit living inside me. New hope and peace entered my heart and mind as I began to draw close to God. I was certain my marriage would be healed now that I was a Christian and faithfully attending church.

To my dismay, John pulled away all the more. His demands for divorce continued as he drilled me with his passion for the party life: not marriage, and not me. I blamed the alcohol, but in a sober moment everything came to a head.

"I want out . . . do you understand, Lisa? I thought being married to you might tame me down . . . but NO! I want a divorce. You say when I hit you it's the alcohol. Smell my breath. Do you smell any alcohol?"

Seated next to him on the couch, I leaned over to sniff his breath. "No," I answered.

With a swift movement, he captured my head in a painful lock and screamed into my ear. "I am totally sober right now!" and he punched my face with a knuckled fist, the blow landing hard under my eye. Pain shot through my body. My cheek and eye swelled immediately.

"That's not alcohol, Lisa," John said. "That's me wanting out of this marriage. Do you get it? I want out of this marriage!"

Despite all this, I still I clung to my naïve hope that we could be a family. I continued to stay with John until late one night he physically threw me out of the house. I stumbled to a filthy telephone booth and called my father.

"Daddy, please come," I begged. "I have to get Shannon out of the house."

In an agonized voice, my father answered, "If you only knew how much it hurts me to see you, my girl, have to go through this. Please let go, Lisa. Stop trying to rescue John . . . or your marriage will end in *'til death do you part* way before it's time."

I hung up the phone and sank to the bottom of the filthy, smelly pay phone booth where people had obviously spit and who knows what else. I felt like I belonged there with that garbage. It was at this time the Lord spoke a loving word into my heart that changed my life forever.

"If your natural father feels that way, imagine how much more I, your heavenly Father, love you and don't want you to suffer."

I felt a shift in my thinking.

I could CHOOSE to believe God. I AM a child of God – not a piece of dirt, not a punching bag. God's intentions for me are good.

That realization gave me the resolve to agree to the divorce John was asking for – before I did end up in a grave.

I remember walking into church after that cataclysmic event sporting a black eye and a smile. I had been emotionally and physically abused, but I had peace and joy. I would not dwell on the past, but cling to the Word that says, "Think on these things . . . things that are lovely, of good report, of virtue . . ."

With the help of the Lord, I refused to listen to the voices of my past telling me I was worthless. Instead, I learned to think on who God tells me I am.

�֎

I flinch when I read of Lisa's abuse. To imagine someone punching my sweet friend is more than I can stand to think about. At the same time, I am inspired because I know the end of her story.

Lisa's friends call her "Smiley Riley," and I don't know any other person who exhibits more joy in her walk with God. She knows her Father loves her and that she is a person of great value. Even her license plate spreads the word of her testimony. It reads, "So Happy" – a sunny contrast to the dark days of physical abuse she experienced.

Many quilt patterns are designed and named after flowers. One popular design is the *Black-Eyed Susan* – a cheerful perennial that looks like a golden daisy with a dark center. As a young girl I sat on the porch of my Kentucky home pulling the petals off these flowers one by one alternating the words "He loves me, he loves me not" as I plucked each petal off. It's a game girls play and a question many women ask.

"Am I lovable?" is the heart of the question for many. As a young woman, I shared Lisa's struggle with self-worth and understanding that God loves me. I hope every reader is encouraged by her story and that we will recall its message with every *Black-Eyed Susan* we see. God *does* love us. We *are* people of worth . . . because of Him. Even when we go through difficult situations, God's unconditional love is always there – reassuring, guiding, and imparting peace and comfort.

And to bring some closure to the story, Lisa eventually remarried a fine, godly man. They had two children together and are now enjoying a new season of life as grandparents.

*Quilts connect the past
with the present and the future.*

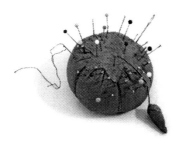

~ 6 ~
Garden Gate
Submitted by Sandra Snider of Minneapolis, Minnesota

"The raspberry is the Cadillac of berries," Don used to say. Affectionately known as the Berry Patch Man, Don was a gentle soul who, each July, opened wide his heavy wooden farm door to the best raspberry patch in town.

Summer after summer, day after day, I drove down the winding gravel road to Don's farm to pay for the privilege of searching through his bushes. Lucky for us, the pickers, the Berry Patch Man charged less for his pints than the groceries, even though his berries were twice the size and sweetness without the "help" of a bit of insecticide. I often insisted he take a couple of extra dollars for all the berries I ate while picking.

Even on the hottest days, the Berry Patch Man wore long denim overalls and a crisp white shirt. Relaxing in a lawn chair under the shade of his truck's canopy, he kept a watchful eye on his pickers who were usually happily chattering about raspberry pies, raspberries on ice cream, or raspberries in cereal. But once out of earshot, the conversations in the prickly rows often turned somber with a familiar, nagging question: what will become of the berry patch when Don dies?

My friendship with the Berry Patch Man grew with each summer's harvest. Over the years, I discovered he wasn't much interested in the Lord. I sometimes mentioned Bible verses to him, which he was always "too busy" to check out; but spiritual issues aside, we enjoyed a special openness in our relationship.

One day Don told me about a large lump in his abdomen. "It's nothing," he insisted. "The doctors are smart and medication will handle it," he said. "A little radiation, a little chemo, and that will be that. I'll be back next year," he assured me as he bent down to encourage one of his littlest pickers with an Oreo© cookie.

He did return the next year, but his worsening condition required more time in the hospital.

"Don might not be around another year," I told a friend who shared my fondness for this gentle man in overalls. We began to pray in earnest: "Please, Lord, don't take Don until he knows You."

That fall I learned the doctors had reached the end of their treatment options. Don was transferred to hospice, where he remained in denial about the severity of his condition. He informed me he was going to get well and return to his farm because he had to prune his bushes and fill in some low spots in the gravel road the rains washed out.

During my visits with Don, I sometimes talked about the Lord. He carefully listened. Each time before I left I asked if he wanted me to pray for him. He always said yes. As I gently rubbed orange-scented lotion on his 80-year old hands and swollen feet, I kept pointing Don to the Lord Jesus, the true Door, according to John 10:9. I wasn't sure how much he understood, but I kept encouraging him to walk through that Door, trade his denim overalls for a white robe of righteousness, and give his sins to Jesus.

"I'm trying," the child in him once said.

Then one day he was agitated and upset. The spiritual atmosphere in his room had changed dramatically, and I became painfully aware of the truth stated in Ephesians 6:12 – that we don't wrestle against flesh and blood, but against principalities and powers of wickedness.

"I've got you figured out," he glared at me. "I know what you're up to. You're concerned about my soul. Well, I'm telling you I'm not going to stand for it, and I won't have it!" I left the hospice center in tears vowing to give Don some emotional and spiritual space.

I stayed away for two full weeks during which I prayed and meditated on Job 33:14-18: "For God may speak in one way, or in another, yet man does not perceive it. In a dream, in a vision of the night, when deep sleep falls upon men, while slumbering on their beds, then He opens the ears of men and seals their instruction. In order to turn man from his deed and conceal pride from man, He keeps back his soul from the Pit and his life from perishing by the sword." (NKJV)

One day the first thought that came to me as I awoke was that I should resume my visits with Don.

"There's just the person I want to see!" Don said with a smile of warm recognition as I approached his bed. "I've been wanting to talk to you and tell you that I think I have a better understanding of things now."

I asked him to clarify, and he said. "I think I've gotten somewhere . . . from there to here. I think I've made some progress."

Was the Berry Patch Man telling me, in his own simple way, that he had prepared himself for eternity? Had something spiritual transferred from his head to his heart? The Bible says in Acts 16:14 the Lord opened the heart of Lydia. Had God opened the heart of our Berry Patch Man and given him wisdom and instruction in an unseen way as he slept?

The Berry Patch Man spent more time sleeping as December's gray days advanced. Eventually, he slipped into a coma. I was with him just two hours before he died a peaceful death.

Today the Berry Patch Man's acreage is owned by his family who has no interest in the raspberry business. The neglected patch is overgrown; Don's experienced, weathered hands will never again prune the bushes. The berries wait to be plucked each July, but the only pickers are hungry birds. And the sturdy farm door that once gave access to hundreds of eager raspberry pickers? It stays securely locked.

Although the wooden door to the berry farm and the portal of time with the dear Berry Patch Man are closed, there is another, far more important Door still open. And I'm hoping a certain raspberry farmer took hold of nail-scarred hands and walked through it.

When I first read Sandra's memories of the Berry Patch Man, I thought, *Great, I'm sure there are lots of quilt patterns about berries and baskets. This will be easy*. But as I edited and read it again, I felt impressed to go another direction and title it *Garden Gate*.

Sandra passed through the rustic door of Don's farm hundreds of times, entering to pick luscious red treasure. But as she filled her belly and baskets with berries, she also made deposits in the life of a humble farmer. As the years passed and her focus shifted from the berries to the Berry Patch Man, Sandra's concern caused her to do a bit of gardening herself – planting a Word here, fertilizing roots there, watering with prayer and pruning with personal encouragement, she tended an eternal plot in Don's soul.

Throughout our days we bump into all kinds of people. At the bank, at the post office, in the grocery, on a kid's ball team – we connect at different levels with the world around us. I pray that every one of us would be sensitive to the opportunities the Lord brings into our lives to let others know, as Sandra shared with the Berry Patch Man, that all have the opportunity to be engrafted into the Kingdom of God. And remember, as we watch for open doors, others are looking at our fruit.

~ 7 ~
Broken Dishes
Submitted by Larry Patton of Troy, Michigan

Tired and hungry after a long day at work, I simply could not face another restaurant meal. I wanted something to eat from home – my home. Standing in the kitchen of my bachelor pad in San Jose, I thought, *A peanut butter and jelly sandwich will hit the spot and hold me over until I can cook something.* I held my right hand steady with my left and managed to get peanut butter on one piece of bread. With the same technique, I started with the jelly on the other.

Diagnosed with cerebral palsy (cp) at the age of two, I daily live with this condition that left me with nerve damage and muscle contractures. My brain does not send proper signals through my nervous system, and I have random, uncontrollable, jerky movements in my extremities and body. The nerves and muscles in my tongue are also affected, making articulation difficult and my speech hard to understand.

Although I had a rewarding career at IBM and managed my disability needs independently, many simple things, like making a sandwich, remained challenging. Basic everyday tasks have always presented a challenge for me, things such as getting dressed, walking, speaking and eating. It may take me several minutes to put on a shirt, even one customized with Velcro closures. When I stand, my legs and feet turn inward, making walking a challenge. The unsteady movement of my arms makes getting food into my mouth difficult.

Fixing a PB&J had seemed a task I could manage – until I wrangled with a contoured glass jelly jar. I was trying to get the

41

uncontrollable rolling movements of my arms timed with dropping jelly on a slice of bread. Just when I scraped a fruity glob to the edge, the jar slipped from my hand and, in what seemed to be slow motion, hit the counter and then smashed on the floor.

I stood staring at the broken glass mixed with sticky jelly splattered across the linoleum and lower cupboard doors. *What a mess!* I thought, realizing what a predicament I was in. This was more than just a sticky mess, the shattered glass posed a significant threat. If I tried to clean it, I was sure to cut my hands when they jerked involuntarily. "How am I going to get this cleaned up?" I asked out loud. I wasn't really expecting an answer, but in an instant, Scott came to mind.

Perhaps if I call him, he would come over to help, I thought. *It's worth a try.*

Dealing with a disability such as cp has caused me to be aware of the feelings of people around me. I won't ask just anyone for help, because I can sense how comfortable a person is or isn't with my disability. I shuffled around the glass shards to the phone on the kitchen wall and dialed Scott's number.

Scott and I were coworkers. I'd only met him briefly when I was first introduced around the office. He seemed an unassuming, compassionate fellow who enjoyed being around people.

One evening I was working late. It was close to 8:00 p.m., and my stomach growled a hungry complaint. Hearing the noise and feeling the rumble, I realized I hadn't eaten since breakfast. I enjoyed my work, and it wasn't uncommon for me to get so engrossed that I worked right through lunch or past dinner.

I got to my feet and headed to the cafeteria for a bite to eat. The route took me past Scott's office, and I noticed he was working late, too. On this particular evening, I decided to take a chance and reach out. Stopping at his lighted office I poked my head in the door and asked, "You want to get a bite to eat?"

"Hey, Larry! I'd love to!" he responded. After purchasing our food we sat across from each other at a cafeteria table, me with my BBQ beef sandwich and Scott with his tuna salad. The conversation flowed comfortably as we shared our stories about how we'd come to work for IBM.

A few minutes into the conversation, Scott began to share on a more personal level. His heart seemed heavy as I studied his face. Behind large, dark-rimmed glasses, I saw his eyes fill with tears. Stopping for a moment to regain composure, he pushed his curly hair off to the side, and began again. He and his wife were separated, and though in some ways it seemed like a good idea, none of the reasons took away the ache inside or the love he still had for his wife of eight years and their three daughters.

Scott was living in a house alone only three miles from my apartment. I dialed the number, hoping he would be available. He was home. I explained my situation and he responded immediately saying, "Larry, I will be right over . . . and uh, thanks for thinking of me."

Within five minutes he was there, cleaning up the jelly and broken glass from my kitchen floor. As I watched him wipe and sweep the linoleum, I was struck with awe at what my Lord had given me at that moment. Here was a friend going through a very difficult struggle of his own, but despite his pain he was reaching out to help me. I saw in Scott Jesus reaching out to me. And I'd thought I would be the one to bring Christ to him.

I stood humbled, soaking in the love of the Lord. I realized for the first time that Jesus cares about *every* detail of our lives – that He is a very personal God. I knew that Jesus suffered and died for my sins, rose from the dead, and will come again for His people, but to think He cares so much about a broken jar of jelly and the damage it could have done to my hands after what he experienced on the cross was a lot to take in. There in my kitchen, I closed my eyes and thanked God for this lesson.

Over the months, it became apparent that Scott was searching for answers in his own life. It was a privilege to be used to speak to him about the Lord. Soon after the jelly jar incident, I was able to share with Scott what Christ had done for him – for us all.

Many months later, Scott and his wife reconciled their marriage and their family was reunited.

�֎

Broken Dishes is a classic pieced design that makes a beautiful quilt or stands alone as a simple block. Each block is comprised of triangles arranged in a four-patch square that are turned at different angles to create a broken dishes effect.

In Larry's story, the individual "blocks" or experiences stand alone in their messages, but also build upon each other creating a beautiful, inspiring pattern.

Block 1: Scott's devastating separation brought him to a place where he interacted with Larry during a late night dinner break baring his hurt and sharing on a deep personal level.

Block 2: In his struggle to live independantly with a physical disability, Larry realized that true freedom comes when he learned to depend on God and the people He brings into his life.

Block 3: A broken jelly jar is the catalyst for a deepening friendship that ultimately reveals God's love to Larry and simultaneously opens the door for Larry to share God's love with Scott.

Block 4: Scott's family is restored as he seeks the Lord for himself and healing for his marriage.

That's the way our God works – piecing unique situations and circumstances together, uniting people for multifaceted purposes in His own divine way. So if your "jelly jar" slips, remember Larry and how he learned that God does care about every detail of our lives. And your lesson may be a blessing to someone else, as well.

~ 8 ~
Sunbonnet Sue
Submitted by Carolyn M. Kenney of Wilmington, Massachusetts

A gaggle of elderly ladies filled the morning air with chattering and laughter. Most were Nova Scotians who moved to our small town in northeastern Massachusetts looking for a better life. Years ago, one by one, as their families moved stateside, the women connected and established new friendships. Sharing their lives and memories in their native tongue, the French Canadian immigrants delighted in the occasional opportunity to spend a day together.

Ninth of ten children, my grandmother, Rose Angeline Surrette, grew up in the remote village of Eel Brook in the late 1800s. The small community east of Yarmouth received its name for the numerous eels in the local river that wound throughout the countryside. A quiet, peaceful place, Grandmother kept memories of her girlhood home close to her heart – memories shared with her twelve friends gathered around the quilting frame in our living room.

Finishing off a quilt was more than a workday gathering, although it certainly was work. Grandmother hosted this day's event, relying on her friends for help. But, as they say, one hand washes the other, and Grandmother would drop everything when one of her friends needed assistance with a project. All the women were eager to share the work load, enjoy each others' company and reminisce about the "good old days."

Well in advance of the quilting bee, Grandmother worked out the details for her new creation. She climbed the stairs to her second-floor bedroom every day for several weeks and lost herself in patchwork and planning. First she selected fabrics pre-cut into an abundance of varying squares, then painstakingly sewed designs in each one: a multicolored flower, or a young child, or a beautiful pattern. She had a keen eye for coordinating colors, and I marveled at the way she combined different hues in contrast and in harmony to create eye-catching blends and motifs.

Quilting bee morn, sons and daughters taxied their mothers to our home. With hugs and greetings in French, Grandmother enthusiastically welcomed each lady at the door. Of course, I hardly understood a word spoken; but, I loved to listen to Grandmother's animated voice and see the joy on her face.

After brief how-do-you-dos, the ladies settled in around a large quilting frame erected in the middle of our living room. The assignment this particular day was to stitch Grandmother's quilt top to its backing. The pattern was one of Grandmother's favorite schemes, a playful little girl named Sunbonnet Sue. Wearing a calico dress and a wide-brimmed hat that hid her face, the fabric image of a girl carrying a watering can adorned the center of the individual squares joined together to make the quilt top. Each lady related to faceless Sue. I imagined any one of them as a young girl carrying the watering can to a kitchen garden or rose bush in Eel Brook or some other pastoral site.

Unsurpassed by machine-work, the craftsmanship of each lady was remarkable and fascinating to watch as nimble fingers guided needle and thread through layers of fabric in precise stitches. And as their fingers diligently wove the needles in and out, merry voices intermingled throughout the house. Hour after hour the friends leaned into their work around the square frame – threading needles with timeworn eyes, starting the thread then methodically running stitches until the thread was used up and tied off. Then starting the rhythm again. And again.

As the ladies worked, Mother prepared a hot meal. She laid out the feast on our dining room table (fully extended with the addition of two leaves) to hold the array of food and accommodate all the chairs. Still laughing and bantering back and forth, the women left their work and gathered around the table. A prayer of thanksgiving and blessing was offered and the meal began – a midday repast of good home cooking, sentimental stories and silly jokes.

Following the meal, the satisfied ladies resumed their positions for several more hours until the workday was called to an end. Tired but smiling, Grandmother escorted each of her friends to the door as respective family members arrived to drive them home. After the door closed behind the last guest, a quiet settled over the house. The look on Grandmother's face was worth all the effort of the day.

Before she passed at the age of 86, Grandmother made an afghan and quilt for many of her 22 grandchildren, including me. Alternating between the two, I place one at the foot of my bed each day. My quilt is large enough to cover a double bed and includes thirty squares. As I spread the quilt on the bed, I affectionately run my hand across it and reflect on the time and care my grandmother spent making it. Four green leaves frame each block of two-tone pink blossoms with yellow centers. Cut from bits and scraps of material, then sewn into a treasure, Grandmother made use of all the "odds and ends" others might have discarded.

Watching Grandmother taught me many lessons: the value of friendship; the pursuit of excellence; loyalty; contentment and faithfulness. And I am truly thankful for the care and attention to detail she gave to a quilt that outlives her days on the earth and continues to convey her warmth and love to her children and grandchildren – love letters written with fabric and thread. Thank you, Jesus, for Grandmother Angie.

Sunbonnet Sue, aka "that girl with the bonnet," is one of the most widely recognized quilt patterns tracing its roots back to the late 1800s. The faceless little girl's antics are memorialized in quilts, watercolors, postcards and other media. She's been depicted, scrubbing and sweeping, watering and walking, washing and ironing, dancing and darning.

Like Carolyn's memories of Grandmother Angie, *Sunbonnet Sue* evokes a nostalgic response of loved ones and days gone by. Every lady can find herself in *Sunbonnet Sue*. She shares with us the routine of life, but she does it in a way that makes us smile. As we face the routine of our days, may we find pleasure in them, knowing God authored each one. And may we, as Carolyn's Grandmother and friends so willingly did, share our lives and talents in ways that bless those around us.

Honeycomb
Submitted by Jeanne Grief of Paducah, Kentucky

It sure is lonely out here on the farm since all my brothers and sisters have gone to new homes. Why haven't I been chosen? Is something wrong with me? A lot of people have come and gone, but I'm still here. Someone called earlier today, but they haven't come. They probably changed their mind.

Oh, here's a car now! There's one . . . two . . . three . . . FOUR little girls, and a lady who looks like she needs a friend; she's so sad. Here come the girls to pet me; I think I'll like them. The lady is looking at me and, what do I see? Oh, can it be? She's smiling as she bends down to pet me. And now, she says it, "Would you like to go home with us?" Wow, would I – girls to play with and a mama to love me.

That car ride was fun, but this place doesn't look like a home. The sign on the door reads *Doctor of Veterinary Medicine*. I've heard of this place; is this some kind of an ugly joke? The lady at the desk is registering me, but I don't even have a name. Mama tells me, "It's okay, we won't hurt you. We need to protect you from those bad germs." Mama lifts me to a cold steel table and here comes the doctor heading straight for me with some BIG needles. I want to go home!

Whee! We're on our way now. "There's our house," one of the girls says. But wait! Stop! We're passing it! What now? Mama has pulled into a driveway down the street, and now she's putting me in an outdoor kennel two doors down from "our house." It's

February; I'm cold and alone again, and it's starting to snow. I thought I was going to a nice warm home with my new family.

Oh, look! I see the back door of "our house" opening. It's Mama, all bundled up against the cold and snow. Here she comes across the neighbors' yards, and she has something in her arms.

She brought a toy, food and water for me. "I wish we could take you inside right now," she says as she tucks me under her warm coat and strokes my head, "but we have to wait a few days so you won't get sick, too. You see, you had a 'brother' who died of old age, and then a 'sister' puppy who was sick with distemper when she came to us, and we have to be sure you're safe against whatever germs are left in the house. We've been so sad, but having you here gives us hope."

Ah, now I understand. Everything is going to be okay. I love my new Mama.

Three days later – I'm going home. As Mama carries me into the warm house I see the girls – my new sisters – and I want to play! There sure are a lot of chew toys around here, but almost everything I like, one of the girls snatches away and says, "No, that's mine." They act like they want to play with me, but they don't want to share their toys.

Mama was tired when she brought me home, and she's in her room resting. I'll just go snuggle up with her for awhile.

What do I hear in the other room? Those girls sound like they're having a lot of fun. I need to check on this.

There they are in a circle in the middle of the floor. Cheryl has a yellow box in her hand and is throwing something from it to each of the other girls. They're eating it!

"I need some of that," I bark, as I worm my way past Lori into the circle for my turn. They must not want to share this with me either, because now they're tossing those tidbits out of my reach. *Well, I'll show them,* I think, as I jump and catch a morsel. That was good, let's do it again. And again. I'm getting good at this. What is this stuff anyway? The box is marked "Honeycomb Breakfast Cereal." There's so much laughter they must be enjoying this as much as I am.

"Look, Mama," Tina says as Mama walks through the door. She tosses another tasty morsel and I catch it in midair.

"Honeycomb," Sandy calls to get my attention as she shows me a piece from the box and tosses it for me to catch.

"I think Honeycomb may be a good name for her," Mama says. Finally, I have a family, a home AND a name. I am so blessed.

Seventeen years later – Mama and I have had quite a life. I've heard people say that a dog is man's best friend, but Mama has been my best friend. I know, because she's always been there for me, too. She told me many times how much she loves me and doesn't know what she would have done without me by her side. We've had a lot of good times, as well as bad times. There have been illnesses, both physical and emotional; my sisters one by one moving out, three of them one by one moving back in, and moving out again; divorce; job changes; five moves – two of which were 600 mile relocations; times of great fun, and times of crushing loneliness. She always took me with her wherever she went. I was there for her through it all, and sometimes I was the only one there.

Now we are back in our hometown. We moved to Grandma and Grandpa's house so Mama could start over again. She has a new job and soon she'll find a new home for us. She is content now with a peace I've never seen in her, so I don't worry about her anymore. She finally got it all together and I know she can get along without me now.

Eight months later – My bones are stiff, yet weak. Laying on this cold steel table is uncomfortable, but it's okay, because Mama is here with me. When she came home from work today, I was not able to move and hadn't eaten for a couple of days. I heard her sob softly as she gently lifted me saying, "I guess it's time to let you go." She brought me to the doctor so he could relieve my pain. As he prepared to put a needle in my vein, I heard him ask Mama, "Do you want to stay, or wait outside?"

I'm so tired. Mama is stroking my head and kissing my nose. Through the tears I hear her say, "If I can't stay with her now, then I didn't deserve the blessings of her loyalty and companionship for all those years. Thank you, Honeycomb. I love you."

"Good night, Mama."

A Word from Mama

We buried my beloved, faithful Honeycomb under a tree on family property the next day. In my lifetime, I have had many pets, but none for so long, or who was so needed as Honeycomb. She came to me at a time when I was having problems dealing with life, and many days I was doing good to get out of bed. People's demands, even my own children's needs, some days, were overwhelming. Honeycomb gave me a reason to go on by happily accepting whatever I was able to give and demanding nothing in return. She had an instinct that told her when I needed comfort and she would nuzzle up against me.

Slowly, as I cared for her, I came out of my darkness and began to care about life again. It's funny how God always provides when we are in need. It may be a person, a situation, or, yes, even an animal who helps us round the corners that lead us in the right direction.

My personal conviction is that it is no coincidence that 'dog' spelled backwards is God. Honeycomb was a perfect example to me of God's unconditional love.

✤

Jeanne Grief was Mama to Honeycomb – and to me. I was one of those little girls. As I researched for this project and came across the name *Honeycomb* in a quilt pattern book, I immediately thought of that shaggy, medium-sized, multicolored mutt my mother loved so much – I didn't know how much until I read her story.

I thank God for throwing the lifeline of a bewhiskered puppy to my drowning mother. I knew she was drowning, but I was just a young girl with little understanding of the emotional struggles she experienced. I just knew I hurt, too. The splashes of a drowning person ripple into the lives of those around them.

I have a lot of happy memories from my childhood, but when I recall the darker days, I praise God the hurt is gone. As one person explained to me, "First you go through a mess . . . then you get a message . . . then you get to be a messenger." So, here I am with the message that God is good and He makes all things beautiful in His time (Ecclesiastes 3:11).

All the little pieces in the *Honeycomb* quilt design are the same hexagon shape and size. The pattern, also called *Hexagon*, features a center piece surrounded by a ring of six pieces in a color contrasting the center piece. The *Honeycomb* pattern was the precursor to the popular *Grandmother's Flower Garden*, which builds on the hexagon shape by adding a third row in another color, then all the flowers are joined by hexagonal rings of a neutral, like muslin. *Grandmother's Flower Garden* became popular during the Great Depression, when ladies laboriously pieced scraps of pastel fabric into cheerful quilts to lift their spirits during hard times.

In the same way the *Honeycomb* pattern became the foundation for *Grandmother's Flower Garden*, I thank God for all He's done for my mother. Mama, now Grandma, has new blooms growing in her garden. There was plenty of fertilizer, so they should look pretty for a right long time!

I love you, Mama. God is good.

*A quilt will warm your body
and comfort your soul.*

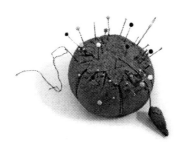

~ 10 ~
Blind Man's Fancy
Submitted by Bernie Lutchman of Chatham, Illinois

He told me a joke! I still can't believe it when I think back on that Tuesday morning almost 20 years ago! My first real encounter with God . . . and He was cracking a joke!

Well, the joke was on me, really. A high-flying, cocktail party kind of guy, I traveled the Caribbean for my job as editor of a tabloid newspaper – a position I landed after graduating from college in Nova Scotia.

A month before my encounter, a severe case of mumps knocked me flat on my back. Depleted from island hopping and partying, my compromised immune system just pooped out.

I lay upon my bed for two weeks evaluating my life in forced solitude. I knew I was living wrong, but hadn't allowed myself to get quiet enough to think about it. In my feverish, weakened condition, all I had was time to think.

My thoughts drifted back to my teen years. I recalled the first sermon I preached in a youth service. I spent hours preparing that first message, and the many that followed. Music replayed in my mind – me strumming my guitar singing about the Lord. And the missions trips – how many? So many memories of all I had done for God, without really knowing Him.

How many services had I attended in my early years? How many Bible verses were spoken in my hearing? How many prayers were said for me – from my own lips and those of others? I knew my mother prayed for me. She made certain I knew it, too. Of course, I didn't welcome her constant reminders, but they didn't really disturb me either. She was truly concerned for my soul. Mother's faith was sincere as she attempted to get my wandering feet on the straight and narrow path.

As a young person, I went through the churchy motions of Christianity, but ritual and mental ascent (even being involved in serving) were not enough to keep me from straying once I was on my own. I shudder to think of the masses of people in our American churches unaware that church attendance or walking down an aisle will not prepare a soul for heaven or keep one from the torment of hell.

Thanks to my moral upbringing, I kept myself from plunging headlong into promiscuous sexual behavior. Alcohol was the demon I chose for my companion. And in all the fellowship with my new friend, I'd forgotten how to pray.

One thing I did remember, however: how to look up Scripture. During my illness, I picked up a Bible and searched for answers to my questions. As I read, my mind was washed and renewed by the Word, and I chose to repent. I made a 180 degree reversal on my path of destruction when I turned to God.

I began talking to Him in prayer, and one morning He visited me. I was sleeping soundly on Tuesday, August 16, 1988. At 4:00 a.m. I felt myself being pulled up the side of a heavily treed mountain. When we finally reached the top, I clearly heard the voice of Jesus. I never saw Him, but I could *feel* His voice full of love. I can say assuredly the Bible is correct: "The voice of the LORD is powerful; the voice of the LORD is full of majesty." (Psalms 29:4) As He spoke, I sensed the smile on His face.

"I have a plan for you," He said.

And then He cracked a joke. I wish I could remember what it was, but I have never been able to recall it. Maybe in heaven I'll remember.

"You're joking with me?" I asked, astonished.

"Who do you think invented a sense of humor?" He replied.

Those words concluded my first face-to-face encounter with the True Living Christ; an event that changed my life. Startled, I jumped out of bed and dressed, but I was not going to spend this momentous day at work. Instead I went to a Benedictine monastery at the top of a mountain in Trinidad. (For some reason, monks like to build on top of dangerous mountains!)

I sat in the monastery's cathedral for hours – confused, blessed, elated, afraid – every emotion a new believer could have – especially one who had been personally visited by Jesus.

As I began serving the Lord, a living God I personally met, He brought wonderful blessings into my life. I married a great girl, the daughter of a Baptist preacher from Alabama. She loves God and has a solid walk with Him.

Referring again to God's sense of humor, I chuckle when I think how the Lord brought a carousing drinker like me into a family that had never touched a drop of alcohol. Over the last two decades, I am thankful to join their ranks in personal prohibition. Ephesians 5:18 says, "And be not drunk with wine, wherein is excess; but be filled with the Spirit."

Beyond a loving, Christian wife, the Lord blessed me with three awesome children who love Him, too – I mean really love Him. What a joy to minister with them wherever God opens the doors, particularly in area nursing homes.

In 2004, I attended a powerful worship service at a Promise Keepers event in St. Louis. I looked up to the rafters and saw what looked like a white cross about four feet high at the top of the assembly of 19,000 men. I rubbed my eyes and looked again. It was still there, transparent and hovering overhead. I continued singing and examining the cross from several angles . . . and it was still there. I stood stunned, wondering if any among the crowd also saw the image as I lifted my hand and saluted the Lord Jesus.

When I was flat on my back, I never imagined the life I enjoy today, but I'm sure I am in good company in that regard. Many years ago God chose a pagan named Gideon to lead His army. In another time, He placed a dirt poor shepherd named David in the Messianic family tree. Billy Graham, a simple dairy farmer's son, impacted Christianity in our millennia. And today, the Lord still reveals Himself in the hearts of His servants, even to a nobody who looks and sounds like me. What an honor to be His.

�֍

An intricate pattern of many triangles and squares, *Blind Man's Fancy* is the quilt pattern that came to mind after reading Bernie's story. Raised in the church, fresh out of college, Bernie allowed himself to be swept into a spiraling vortex of sin. Blinded by the "pleasure of sin for a season," he sought after his own fancy – the great deception of satan. But God – oh, how I love those words – but God had other plans for Mr. Lutchman.

Although Bernie forgot how to pray, his mother's prayers were fragrant incense continually burning before the Lord. God heard the desperate pleas for her son and reached out in great mercy to His lost lamb. One encounter with Jesus, and deception's scales fell from Bernie's blinded eyes.

I'm sure Bernie would tell you today that through his ordeal he learned this great truth: pleasure-seeking never satisfies a God-empty heart; but God-seeking brings pleasure and a satisfied heart.

And, moms and dads, don't stop praying for your lost lambs.

~ 11 ~
Grandma's Fan
Lori Wagner

Normal is only a setting on your clothes dryer . . . or so I've heard. When it comes to families, mine certainly wasn't and isn't anything close to what I consider "normal."

Relatives on both sides of the family have suffered from mental illness. Although it wasn't openly talked about, I know of multiple suicide attempts by people very close to me as well as serious diagnosed mental conditions and hospitalizations.

A reclusive genius, my great uncle only spoke to my sisters and me through his screen window, his head turned away so we couldn't see his face. When I think of it now I flash back to closed confessional experiences from parochial school days – where the priest offered absolution and blessing from behind his curtain.

Between the two of them, Mama and Daddy participated in six marriages, and that's only counting their marriage to each other once. The tidal shifting of spouses distributed a continuing seismic upheaval of steps, halfs and exes further complicating our turbulent lives. And the pit in the cherry of the melting banana split of my youth was when not one, but two of my stepfathers had inappropriate physical relationships with me. I left home to make it on my own at an early age.

Considering the magnitude of the dysfunction, it's good to look beyond the chaos and brokenness and remember one shining source of stability. My grandma was that for me. Oh, I know she was not a perfect person. I'm certain things discussed outside my hearing might stain my rosy view of her, but as her granddaughter, I can tell you what a positive impact her day-to-day life had on me.

Growing up, Sundays were for going to Grandma's house, after Mass, that is. Grandma and Grandpa lived in a quiet town in a home designed and built by Grandpa's own hands. Grandpa served in World War II, and he and his bride began their marriage in difficult financial times. Grandma learned to pinch a penny until the copper melted between her fingertips and cried out for mercy.

In the security of my grandparent's home, children played with baby dolls sporting shocks of matted hair and rigid "skin" discolored with age. They weren't pretty, but they were clean, and Grandma kept them just for us, so that made them special even though they were old. Over the years she amassed quite a collection of empty spools in a box in the kitchen cabinet. Everyone loved to play with those old wooden spools.

There were other play things like Lincoln Logs©, Tinker Toys© and board games. I remember gathering around The Game of Life© with my siblings and cousins as we created our own little families of peg people driving plastic cars around the colorful game board. We took turns spinning the wheel to see what life would bring in our attempts to retire in ease at Countryside Acres. It seems ironic now looking back and realizing how very many "real life" lessons we learned at Grandma's, not even noticing as we idled away our childhood days in her home.

Grandma's frugality is an attribute that lives on in our family memories. My Uncle Tony loves to talk about her thriftiness. He and his family live out of town and visited once or twice a year. On one of his stays, he ordered in pizza for dinner. Upon his return a year later he was very surprised to see Grandma serve him pizzeria pizza. "Where'd you get this, Mom?" he asked, only to be astounded by her raspy reply, "I saved it from the last time you were here." She'd frozen the leftovers and presented them proudly a year later!

I've heard that when my uncles came to visit, they routinely gave Grandma $20 bills upon entering the front door, then proceeded directly to the thermostat to adjust the heat or air conditioning to comfortable levels.

Once my sister and her roommate shared dinner with Grandma only to discover she had prepared frozen mixed vegetables packaged 20 years prior. Seriously! They dug the bag out of the garbage and checked the expiration date. "What are these white things?" my sister asked in her initial attempt to ascertain the origins of her meal. It took some time, but they finally figured out that what looked like potatoes were in fact albino carrots. In their old age, the vegetables had blanched pale white, but Grandma would not back down. "They're still good," she insisted, though I heard she maintained her ground behind a silly smirk. I think she knew she'd crossed the line that time.

My grandma could sew. She could make anything out of anything, and nothing went to waste. Curtains, clothes, dolly dresses and wedding dresses, afghans and quilts were bestowed by giving hands to those around her.

Each year she planted a garden and put up its yield of fruits and vegetables. Her green beans were famous, and I have a memorial jar of them in my kitchen that I can't bring myself to eat, even though I know practical Grandma would rather they were eaten than "unused."

Because she was so frugal and worked diligently with her hands, Grandma was able to do things she would not have been able to otherwise. She and Grandpa had six children, each of whom married at least once. Just one of their daughters had ten children. We're talking a big family! And then the grandchildren started marrying and having children. That was a lot to keep track of.

It's hard to believe, but Grandma never, I mean NEVER missed a birthday or Christmas – for me, my husband, or my children. Sure, you might not have selected for yourself the t-shirt she purchased from the St. Vincent De Paul Society (with the manufacturer's tag still on it), but it's the thought that counts, right? When I was a teenager, she'd send me $2 in a card and tell me to treat myself to a burger from McDonald's. Grandma always kept track of me, even as I crisscrossed the country concurrently looking for myself and running away from myself in a whirlwind of bad choices. She never lost touch, but pursued me with her love, even when I chose to separate myself from many of my relatives.

Through the years people drifted in and out of the family unit – roommates and wanderers, new babies, stepchildren and foster children, even spouses entered and exited through the loss of death and divorce. Grandma included everyone in her heart and her gift giving. And I'm telling you, it wasn't the gifts. It was that she made you feel part of the family, accepted – even wanted. That's something my heart has always treasured.

In so many ways, my grandma exemplified the Proverbs 31 woman. Following are some excerpts.

Who can find a virtuous woman? Her price is far above rubies. She . . . worketh willingly with her hands . . . she planteth a vineyard. She layeth her hands to the spindle . . . She stretcheth out her hand to the poor; yea, she reacheth forth her hands to the needy. Strength and honour are her clothing; and she shall rejoice in time to come. In her tongue is the law of kindness. She looketh well to the ways of her household, and eateth not the bread of idleness. Her children arise up, and call her blessed; her husband also, and he praiseth her. Let her own works praise her

God gave me a very precious gift the last time I was able to be with Grandma. My husband and I rented a houseboat on Kentucky Lake and invited our family in the area to join us for dinner on board. It was a beautiful time on a peaceful lake with good food, smiling kids, fishing, visiting and singing along as my sister strummed familiar tunes on her acoustic guitar. Grandma volunteered to bring dessert, and she made apple pies from scratch with fruit from the trees in her yard. I can still see the boxes she recycled to carry those pies in. The image is burned into my memory along with a picture of her laughing with her family gathered around her at the table on the boat.

Only three weeks after we returned home, Grandma became ill and soon died. My sister wrote the following tribute which I was honored to read at her funeral.

Grandma's House

Graham cracker treats
At the bar on her stool
The old apple tree
And playing with spools
No place else in the world
Was quite like Grandma's house

The ping pong table
Was for supper and fun
And each family gathering
Brought new little ones
Into the wonderful world of Grandma's house

Both strangers and visitors
Were just like family
And at Christmastime too
Found their names under her tree
Where else I wonder now
But at Grandma's house

Yes such busy hands
Quilting and sewing
Snapping green beans
And not even knowing
The memories she was making for all
At Grandma's house

~ Cheryl Lee Yates, 09/07/03

�֎

To some, Grandma's days may seem to have been quite simple or even mundane, like the beige or uninteresting pieces of a quilt top. Thoughts of Grandma stir up refreshing memories of her love and acceptance in my soul – propelled by remembrances of her many acts of kindness and simple expressions of love. I'm reminded of the quilt pattern, *Grandma's Fan*, when I think of my grandmother's benevolent deeds and caring ways fanning out through time and generations, continuing to refresh the lives of those she touched even after her passing.

She never scaled Kilimanjaro. She never started a business, wrote a book or did any really "big" thing; but the love and unconditional acceptance she poured into the lives of her family circle were huge. I needed it then, and now I need to exemplify that in my life as I relate to others.

So on the days when the routine is oh-so-routine, and the beige days of life are oh-so-very-beige, remember that it's the little choices and the little things that can be a source of stability and blessing in the lives of others. Embrace the opportunities to affirm those around you, even if the methods seem small and insignificant, because if it touches someone's heart, it's not simple or small at all.

~ 12 ~
Evening Star
Submitted by Cristina Broomfield of Troy, Michigan

The passing of time seems contingent upon the events of the moment. When there are lots of errands to be done, time seems to run out. On the other hand, when we are waiting to hear news – good or bad – time creeps by at an unbearably slow pace.

Waiting in a special room with the hospital chaplain for news of my youngest daughter's condition was excruciating. My husband and I received a call around 3:00 a.m. on a hot Sunday morning in August. We rushed to the hospital, but after arriving were unable to get any information because we hadn't yet met the attending physician. Of course, the doctor couldn't meet with us because he was busy treating our daughter. So we waited, and time stood agonizingly still.

As I waited, my thoughts traveled back to the morning I delivered this precious baby. Her name was already picked out – Adam, my first son. But I realized God had different plans as I held my third little girl in my arms just moments after her delivery. She was beautiful!

Yet life was not so beautiful for this little one. I first discovered her struggle with depression when she asked me, "Mom, what does it feel like to be happy?" She was only 12 years old. Behavior during middle school began to reveal my child was self-medicating. Her drug of choice was alcohol.

The behavior escalated during high school until one night she attempted to take her own life. Her dad and I were desperate for help and began the tenuous journey of inpatient care facilities, antidepressants, therapists, and of course, prayer.

I snapped back to reality as I was finally ushered into the trauma unit. The face of my once lovely daughter was unrecognizable. Lacerations covered her lips and forehead. A breathing tube protruded from her mouth and was taped over her bleeding lips. A mixture of dried blood and yellow antibacterial lotion covered her forehead and matted her hair. Only jagged ends of porcelain were left of her front teeth, and her left leg was gigantic, wrapped in thick bandages. She was unconscious. I was numb.

It took ten days before she finally opened her eyes and responded to any stimuli. We almost lost her twice. The final medical assessment listed a broken left femur, crushed pelvis, shattered left knee-cap and a closed head injury. The police report revealed even worse news. My daughter had been drinking at a friend's house after a fight with her estranged husband and went out to make a phone call. On the return trip from the corner pay phone, she darted across the street and was struck by an SUV. The driver had also been drinking. Two lives collided that night, and the result changed the course of so many more.

Not long after the incident I found myself sitting at the kitchen counter alone. Raising my arms to heaven I cried out, "Why God?" My voice was barely audible as I struggled with the horrific pain pounding inside my chest. "Take all that I have, God – take my home, my bank accounts, my degrees, my health – but give me back my daughter!"

I wanted her back – my baby girl who loved to climb up in my lap and twirl my hair until it knotted. The toddler that tromped behind me planting her footsteps in mine in the snow. The brave little girl who rescued her two older sisters from an enormous spider daring to invade their toy chest.

I thought I would die of a broken heart that afternoon. I could not fathom why God had allowed this to happen. I'd gone to Bible school and served the Lord in full-time ministry since I was 24 years old. The grief and mourning was so heavy I felt I would suffocate under it. Why wasn't God listening?

I began questioning what I thought I knew of God. If He was truly loving, why would He allow all the suffering that goes on in the world? The question plagued my soul. At every turn of my daughter's recovery process I looked for answers from God. "Will she finally give her life to You, Lord?" "Will all this suffering cause others to come to know and believe in You?" "Will this horrific experience draw our family closer together?"

Silence.

Attending church services was a challenge I barely managed. I had always been strong. I felt that letting others know how much I was hurting was not something I could do. Yet, I could not stop the tears. A simple question from a distant friend would send me spinning downward. My solution was keeping my church family at a distance, so I withdrew from them – and from God as well. After all, I reasoned, He wasn't listening anyway.

I began a journey to the depths of Hell without companionship from God. It was a path of total despair. Without hope. Without a promise of deliverance – only a deep void that haunted me every moment of every day. Despite my questions and God's silence, I could not stay away from Him long. Although I still felt angry and abandoned, I ran back to my Father. It was only then that I began to sense His presence and feel His love again.

Over time I gained new understanding of why God allows suffering in the world. I learned that while we live in a world created by God, we also live in a world given over to the evil one. John 11 records Jesus' response at hearing that His dear friend Lazarus died. The Scripture tells us "When Jesus saw her (Mary) sobbing and the Jews with her sobbing, a deep anger welled up within him. He said, Where did you put him? Then Jesus, the anger again welling up within him, arrived at the tomb." The story goes on to share how Jesus raised Lazarus from the dead. However, it was the anger part that spoke volumes to me.

I believe that Jesus was angry with the human condition. Because of the entrance of sin in the world, people experience sickness, heartache, and death. None of this comes *from* God. Because of sin we are destined to face a world filled with every sort of evil. Jesus' heart breaks at the state of our human condition and as He witnesses His people falling prey to the evil one. But until our Lord's return, our hearts and lives are vulnerable to experience depths of pain that can at times knock us to our knees.

It is there, on our knees, that we will find the strength to endure. While many shake their fists in the face of God, blaming Him for their pain, I have learned to shake my fists in the face of the evil one, claiming the promise that my God will make sense out of all the suffering my family has had to endure. I have also learned to turn my face upward, not downward. I have learned that while I may not "hear" God, He is still there in the midst of my circumstances. He is waiting for me to crawl up in His lap and bury my heart in His chest. It is there that He turns my sorrow into peace.

It would be wonderful if I could conclude this chapter with a testimony that God has finally revealed the reasons He allowed such pain to enter my daughter's life and the lives of my family. It would be a glorious conclusion if I could tell you she has come back to her faith, she has stopped the use and abuse of alcohol, and she currently speaks to church groups about her life changing experience.

But that is not the case. The struggles continue, but so does the refinement of lives through the power of faith. This story goes on, and the lives this tragic experience touched continue to go through the fire.

In Daniel 3:13-30 Scripture tell us the story of three young men cast into the fiery furnace after their refusal to bow down to a man. Not only were these three young men delivered through an impossible fire by a faithful God, their garments did not even smell of smoke (v.27).

There is no greater pain than to watch your child experience a life void of God's presence. However, the greater tragedy is to allow the evil one to gain access to your own life and cause you to live in daily defeat. This is true bondage.

Living in the fire, knowing that full deliverance has already taken place through Jesus Christ, removed the smell of smoke from my life. The squalid scents of anger, depression and crushed dreams were swept away by a faithful God when I claimed His promises in the Word and held on tight. While circumstance may not change, sometimes even worsening, it is God who asks us to allow Him to write the last chapter of our lives . . . and the lives of our children.

※

Although it is only a planet, Venus shines as a silvery-white star-like object. When adorning the western sky, the planet bears the name Evening Star as it shines brilliant light in the darkness. However, this phenomenon lasts only for a season.

As Venus overtakes the earth on its orbit of the sun and begins appearing in the eastern sky, the bright planet that once heralded the sunset begins a new role announcing the coming of day. It dominates the predawn sky with its glorious heavenly light and receives a new name: the Morning Star.

Evening Star is a beautiful nine-patch quilt pattern. It has a solid middle piece, representing the planet Venus, then features triangular patches radiating out from the center. I titled Cristina's story *Evening Star*, because although she still lives with the darkness of her daughter's struggle, she relies upon the beacon of hope God's comforting Word shines into her night.

As I read her story, I pictured the orbit shifting from the western sky to the eastern sky as she ran back into her heavenly Father's arms recommitting her life and that of her daughter again to the Lord. And as you and I pray with her, we watch for the predawn light proclaiming the coming of the morning for her family. Until that time, may we all be encouraged by her faith and transparency in dealing with this traumatic situation.

When life throws you scraps
. . . make a quilt.

~ 13 ~
"Rose of Sharon"
Submitted by Melissa May Hoffmann of Rochester Hills, Michigan

Mrs. Roshak lived behind me when I was growing up. She was tall and incredibly skinny with jet-black hair and beautiful lily-white skin – her only makeup the reddest of red lipsticks. Mrs. Roshak's energy was remarkable. Toiling in her garden or hanging out laundry, she glided from task to task so fluid in her transitions an observer had to watch carefully to notice when she exchanged a rake for a bag of clothespins.

As memorable as her physical traits were, what indelibly imprinted Mrs. Roshak in my heart and mind was an entirely different attribute. Mrs. Roshak personified what being a good neighbor is all about – and she did it with banana bread.

The initial loaf came after my mother was diagnosed with breast cancer. Mom was home recuperating from a radical mastectomy when Mrs. Roshak knocked on the back door. My brother opened it and received the first of the loaves destined to be part of our lives over the next several years.

There was something magical about Mrs. Roshak's banana bread that I can't really describe. The aroma was this incredible nutty banana buttery mixture – the crust an even brown, the inside tan with black flecks. My siblings and I murmured our pleasure as our taste buds exploded in delight with each bite. The loaves never lasted long. We devoured them within minutes and whoever wasn't home when they arrived . . . well, better luck next time.

What made the bread so delicious is something I revisit from time to time. Perhaps because four children under the age of fifteen were making the family meals and everything tasted like fried leather. Or could it be the nature of the giver; her kind and selfless ways? My mother loved Mrs. Roshak, maybe that was it. Her words were genuine and her concern for our situation was real. The bread she gave us was as sincere as its baker – and that transmitted into the taste buds of four children, nourishing us with all that is good about humankind.

Mom's cancer continued to advance. She endured stays in the hospital lasting several months. This put more responsibility on my older sister and brother to care for the household. Dad spent all his free time with Mom. When he was not with her, he was researching and challenging the medical world for answers. We all struggled, but seeing Dad with a broken heart was almost as hard as watching our mother slip away.

The day was always brighter when we saw Mrs. Roshak bounding across the lawn with a foil wrapped package of freshly made banana bread. Her acts of kindness, although small perhaps in Mrs. Roshak's mind, meant so much more to us than just slices of bread. One of the ways she impacted our lives was by providing the seeds of being a good neighbor. These seeds carried into our adulthood, and I have never underestimated their value. Pearls of wisdom delivered in tin foil, her actions revealed that it does not take much to show compassion – a simple loaf of bread will do!

Her lipstick always in place, her movements fluid as a river, her voice soft like the butter she used to bake the bread, Mrs. Roshak taught us unaware. That was never her motive – she never preached. Sometimes she would knock on the door, leave the loaf and dash off. Other times she would come in the house and talk with my mother, first propping her pillows, then moving on to clean the kitchen or fold the clothes five days out of the dryer crumpled in a basket.

When my mother died, the lives of our family members changed dramatically. Mom's cancer had been our focus, and other than school, my siblings and I spent all our time together. It felt strange to let go of each other and enter the world again. We stayed together after mom died, but soon it was time to move on. One thing was constant; however, Mrs. Roshak's banana bread continued in a steady stream, its taste now conjuring a different meaning, but still delicious all the same.

My father was 42 years old and not ready to be alone. After a time, he began dating. We took him shopping for new clothes, and my brother tried to "hip" him up so he would fit into the singles scene. It was fun to meet his girlfriends and see Dad acting romantic. Eventually he found the love of a good woman, Jackie, and when they announced their engagement, we were elated. She was ten years younger than Dad, gentle, kind and just what we needed to be a whole family again.

After Dad remarried, Mrs. Roshak's banana bread tapered off, but never stopped completely. She brought a loaf over to welcome Jackie to the neighborhood and another when my little sister was born. The bread's meaning always changing, but its taste still defying description, my family never forgot its constant presence in our lives.

When I am in the area, I like to drive through my old neighborhood. I pass slowly in front of the old house and immerse in the memories. One day I saw Mrs. Roshak out walking her dog. We caught ourselves up on family happenings, and as we parted, I asked her if she still made banana bread. "You know, not in many years," she said.

Through my tears, I expressed to Mrs. Roshak how much those loaves meant to my family. She hugged me for a long time, told me how much she loved my parents, and that she thought we were the bravest children she had ever met. Her words were sincere and soothing, just like her bread from all those years ago. I tried to soak in all the goodness of Mrs. Roshak as we parted knowing I would never see her again. I watched her scurry down the street for a long time before I pulled away.

It has been over 25 years since I have tasted Mrs. Roshak's banana bread. When I bake for my family, my husband and children ask me about the legend of Mrs. Roshak. My sisters and I searched the world over for a recipe comparable to hers. We never hit the mark, but then we are staunch critics. I think I have come close with one recipe, and that is the one I use on a consistent basis. It doesn't seem to have the power to transform human emotions, but it will have to do.

Over the years I have delivered several loaves to neighbors – some who lost loved ones, some celebrating the birth of a child, and one to a neighbor diagnosed with cancer. It is no doubt a small act, worth a thank you and not much more, but I do it primarily for one reason: Mrs. Roshak. I honor Mrs. Roshak and her Christ-like spirit every time I bake and deliver a loaf of banana bread, always hoping that somehow its taste will provide respite to the recipient, just as it did for my brother, my sisters and me all those years ago.

�֍

Through the words of one she touched by her kindness, I imagine Mrs. Roshak as a lovely and fragrant rose brightening the thorn-laden trial Melissa's family endured – an elegant red rose on an old fashioned rosebush from an era gone by.

Researching the *Rose of Sharon* quilt pattern, I discovered the traditional color palette is red and green on a white background. Most designs feature a large center flower with four smaller ones shooting out from or circling around the larger center one. Looking at the quilt blocks, I thought of Mrs. Roshak reaching out to the four children in Melissa's family – even dropping seeds into their lives where new plants would eventually grow, bloom and bless the lives of others. In her kindness, Mrs. Roshak exemplified the true Rose of Sharon, Jesus Christ, reaching out to the hurting with compassion and love.

~ 14 ~
Mariner's Compass
'Submitted by Eileen Kruper of Troy, Michigan

In August 1995 I took advantage of a rare opportunity. My friend had a cottage in the woods overlooking a quiet lake, and she gave me the use of it. Two to three days all to myself would be worth the three-hour drive north.

At the time, I desperately needed some solitude. My husband and I were concerned with the choices our daughter, 16, and son, 20, had been making. Each was choosing a destructive path and neither would heed our admonitions. We'd always been a close family, so the tension-filled atmosphere in our home during the past months had been a great strain. My husband and I prayed for direction and I especially prayed for release from the continual anxiety that plagued me.

Yes, I longed to get away for a while, and my husband agreed it would be good for me to go. He assured me he'd come home early so our daughter (likely to sleep late while I was away) wouldn't have too much time on her own.

Always finding it a challenge to be ready for a trip on time, I promised myself to leave no later than 5:00 p.m. I'd be driving alone in an unfamiliar area, so I wanted to arrive at the cottage before nightfall. But habits die hard. All day I kept up a steady pace of laundry, dishes, errands, phone calls, etc., while intermittently putting things in a suitcase.

The heat and humidity were oppressive, never dipping below the mid-90s. Our home was not air-conditioned, but we did have a backyard pool. I took a few minutes out for a quick swim, submerged myself completely several times, and stretched out in a relaxing float. It kept me cooler the next couple of hours as I hurried from one task to another.

As my deadline for departure approached, I was just starting to throw together a meal. *Well, they have to eat,* I reasoned, *and so do I. Anyway, now I won't have to stop for a bite along the way.* By the time I pulled out of the driveway it was nearly 7:00 p.m. The ever-present anxiety asserted itself more acutely at the awareness I would never make the cottage before dark. I uttered a prayer for protection then focused my attention on the road.

My thoughts turned to how I'd planned to spend this precious "alone" time at the lake. I hoped to communicate with God more closely than seemed possible at home with so many duties and distractions. He seemed so distant. I'd prayed many months for peace and freedom from fear, mostly about my children. Relational problems with them were ongoing, and the future looked grim. After prayer, peace came, but only momentarily. I struggled with doubts about my very faith in God and in myself as a mother. *Where are you, Lord? You promised to be with us in our time of suffering. Why don't I feel Your presence?*

Settling into the freeway traffic moving out of the suburbs, I switched on the radio. *Focus on the Family* was in progress and Dr. Dobson was speaking with several women who had survived breast cancer. One of them explained how depressed she got at times feeling she might die with all her hopes and dreams lost forever. But then she remembered where it says in the Bible ". . . though there are no sheep in the pen and no cattle in the stalls, yet I will rejoice in the Lord." When she took a breath, Dr. Dobson continued the passage from memory. "The Sovereign Lord is my strength; He makes my feet like the feet of a deer, He enables me to go on the heights." *How uplifting,* I thought, and made a mental note to find those verses when I got settled at the cottage. I'd never heard or read that passage of Scripture before. A Christian for many years, I was a relative newcomer to serious Bible study.

Soon, ominous clouds gathered and the sky ahead became increasingly dark. The rain began to fall and concerns about safety welled up within me again. *Oh, why hadn't I left earlier? I probably could have avoided this downpour if I'd had my act together and left on time.*

I remembered a tape my husband received at a Promise Keepers gathering and pushed it into the tape deck. The music was lovely. I'd listened to it several times before. The words were so meaningful, and I soon joined in singing the familiar songs completely absorbed in praise.

After many miles I realized I'd forgotten the unnatural darkness and sloshing of the windshield wipers. The rain was subsiding. I glanced up to see a glorious break in the western sky, and the view was breathtaking. The brooding clouds, which darkened the entire sky, parted to reveal a large area of bright blue. Some wispy clouds drifted across the opening reflecting pink from the light of the hidden, setting sun.

This striking contrast to the darkness all around filled me with wonder as the praise music continued to envelope me. A feast to my eyes and ears all at once, it comforted my troubled spirit. *Perhaps God is trying to get my attention,* I thought. *Maybe he's telling me that things on the home front aren't as gloomy as they appear.*

After leaving the freeway, I traveled many miles of narrow road flanked by dense woods on either side. It was now very dark. Nearing the lake there was an unmarked turn I feared I might pass by. But, prayers answered, I pulled up to the cottage at about 10:15 p.m. without missing a single turn.

It was still raining lightly, but I had no trouble getting my things inside. After locking up I finally felt some of the tension slip away. I called home as promised, then prepared for bed, having decided to spend a short time in prayer and devotion before settling down to sleep. I propped myself up with pillows – a lighted lamp and my Bible and devotional booklet beside me. It was nearing midnight. The air was decidedly cooler, but under the blankets I felt snug and comfortable as I reached for the booklet.

77

I remembered my desire to find the verses I'd heard on the radio earlier. It was late so I thought I'd do my scheduled reading and look for it in the morning. Opening the booklet, I turned to Wednesday, August 16, and noted the reading for the day was Habbakuk 3:17-19. Finding it in the Bible, I began to read. "Though the fig tree does not bud and there are no grapes on the vine, though the olive crop fails and the fields produce no food, though there are no sheep in the pen and no cattle in the stalls, yet I will rejoice in the Lord . . ." Recognition coming over me, I caught my breath and read on. "I will be joyful in God my Savior. The Sovereign Lord is my strength; he makes my feet like the feet of a deer, he enables me to go on the heights." (NIV)

Oh, my! How could this be? I turned to the back of the book. *There are 1,100 pages in my Bible. Surely, there are many thousands of verses here!* A chill fell upon me. My eyes suddenly moist, I got out of bed and walked slowly through the darkened rooms. An indescribable sensation of euphoria came over me. For several minutes the Spirit of God embraced me and coursed through my entire being as I contemplated His presence. Never before, or since, have I experienced anything even remotely similar.

If God opened the sky to give me hope earlier, I had received the grace, but my tension had only been momentarily displaced. Now He made certain that I would take notice by leading me to the very words I needed, but might never have found on my own. He was surely confirming that in spite of the difficulties with my children, He is my strength, and I can be joyful. Even with black and sinister clouds all around me, He is the bright, blue sky I can see beyond them.

Now, no matter what twists and turns the road ahead may bring, or what storms may gather, I can trust Him for a happy outcome, and take joy in His presence along the way.

❁

The *Mariner's Compass*, one of the oldest documented quilt patterns, dates back to 1726 New England. The pattern features a star design of 16 to 32 points that emanate from a circular center, unlike other star designs where the points radiate from center squares. The pattern brings to mind days gone by – when captains wearing beplumed hats guided tall ships across the high seas – days of parchment nautical charts decorated with ornate drawings of mariners' compasses.

In God, we have a guide Who existed before the creation of any navigational instruments, and yet Who directs unfailingly the steps of His people. He created the earth with a magnetic field that turns every compass needle northward. Likewise, God created man with a "magnetic" pull to His "true north."

True north is a navigational term that, as other compasses, refers to the direction of the North Pole; however, it is relative to the navigator's position. In other words, depending on where you are, your true north arcs a bit differently than someone else's.

With reference to the earth's axis, true north is determined by the fixed spot of the North Pole. A Christian's true north, the fixed, immovable point of reference, is the throne of God – Heaven's true north.

Natural and spiritual storms assailed Eileen as she traveled to her rendezvous with the Lord. God not only kept Eileen safe on her journey, but He spoke words to her anxious heart, giving her the direction and hope she needed to face her situation with confidence and peace.

The Lord directs us with the aid of many different methods. He speaks directly into our hearts. He brings people into our lives who give us wise counsel. The most sure way, I believe, is when He uses His Word – the infallible, unchanging, Word. His Word is a lamp to our feet, lighting the path before us – a sure compass pointing our hearts to the Lord's true north.

May your sorrows be patched,
May your joys be quilted,
May your bobbin always be full.

~ 15 ~
East to Eden
Submitted by Suzanne Stoltz of Rolla, Missouri

My years in elementary school reached their zenith at an official sixth grade graduation ceremony. One by one, my scrubbed and polished classmates crossed the stage to receive diplomas indicating their new status as middle-school students. As the teacher called each name, she also announced what the graduate wanted to be when he or she grew up. I had given little consideration to her question earlier in the year, never imagining my teacher would share my response with a room full of people.

"Suzanne Nash . . . wants to be a missionary in China." Somewhat rattled by her proclamation, I walked to my teacher, shook her hand, grasped my diploma and looked across the room filled with surprised people – including my parents. Why, even I had a hard time believing my ears. My actions at school and home were not what you would expect from an aspiring missionary – my nature not what you would call Christ-like.

I mentioned China to my teacher because when she asked the question of what I wanted to be when I grew up, I had recently seen the movie "The Inn of the Sixth Happiness." In the film Ingrid Bergman played a missionary who served in China in the 1940s. The depiction of the true story of Gladys Aylward made such an impact on my life that after seeing it, I wanted to be a missionary to China.

Ironically, I was not saved at the time of my declaration, although I attended church with my family and prayed daily.

But God knows the end from the beginning, and I believe He put a love in my heart at a young age for the Chinese people and their country. Typical of most sixth graders, the magnitude of the commitment and sacrifices required by missionaries escaped my understanding. When I reached adulthood, I realized how hard it would be to accomplish my childhood dream. Only God could make that happen.

In 1972 I gave my life to the Lord. Married with a one-year-old son, I was certain I would never make it to China.

Several years later, my son Jeff made friends with a little Taiwanese boy named Frank. They attended the same nursery school, and our families started getting together for play dates after school. Frank's mother Tricia and I became very close, and I was able to share the Lord with her. She gave her life to God and asked me to share the gospel with her husband Phillip who also accepted the Lord. With joy I realized that God had fulfilled my dream of witnessing to the Chinese people.

God blessed me with two more children, Deborah and Christen. Many years passed, but eventually the Lord provided another opportunity for me to minister to the Chinese. In 1997 my husband and I became host parents to two University of Missouri-Rolla students from China. We shared the Lord with them and their wives, and they became Christians. They attended church with us, and over time we added more Chinese students.

A professor's wife and I started a Bible study at the University housing in the Chinese section. God blessed our efforts and many of the students gave their lives to the Lord. The students often led their parents to Him, as well. Thankfully, a Chinese church in the area helped them grow in the Lord. For the Chinese students away from their families, we gave baby and wedding showers and hosted baptisms, Christmas and Thanksgiving dinners and birthday parties to provide for their needs.

In 2001, the University of Missouri-Rolla offered me a job coordinating a Friends Program. This program connects community members to new students. Families befriend foreign students, meeting with them on a regular basis and taking them to activities and their homes so they can get a feel for the American lifestyle. I matched students with local families and organized a reception for them to meet. Around 100 families each took from 1 to 4 students. I had over 20 students from several countries.

The University hired me to travel overseas recruiting students. I also helped alumni start sections (a type of fraternity for alumni) in their native countries. Through my secular job, I was able to share my faith with people from around the world – people from Singapore, Thailand, Hong Kong, Taiwan, China, Turkey, Malaysia and Indonesia.

The Chinese Consulate General in Chicago, Jiacai Cheng, came to Rolla to meet me and the others helping the UMR Chinese students. He heard about all the showers, parties and dinners and wanted to personally thank us for the support and assistance we provided the Chinese students. Some time after his visit, I traveled to Chicago and met with Jiacai, his wife and son over dinner. We talked about my dream to go to China, and he said he had all the connections to help me – to give him a call when I was ready to go.

Seated around Jiacai's dinner table sharing my dreams with his family, I never imagined the Lord would use this relationship to arrange my first trip to China. Jiacai previously worked for the Chinese Service Center for Scholarly Exchange (CSCSE), an organization specializing in a full range of services for international scholarly exchanges. This connection provided the perfect opportunity for me to meet with and introduce the abstinence program to the CSCSE for consideration in the entire Chinese school system. Jiacai even sent a visa for me.

I flew to China (my dream come true) and met with a number of CSCSE department leaders to discuss the program. The Lord gave me favor, knitting our hearts together. Upon my return to the States, I made arrangements with the staff at Focus on the Family who were thrilled the CSCSE leaders wanted to have their abstinence program in every school in China. I returned to China with the Focus staff who presented their program to the CSCSE.

When we finished, we were taken to Shijiazhuang, Hebei Province, to see where the project would start.

Looking back on the experience, I would say my greatest joy was sharing from 1 Corinthians 13. The people had never heard the "Love Chapter." Unaware they were listening to text from the Holy Bible, the beauty of the phrases captivated them and they asked for my paper to give to their daughters. The people were hungry for God's Word and His presence.

I traveled to Shanghai, Beijing, Yu Yuan, Wu Xi, Su Zhou, Harbin and Daqing. I saw the Great Wall, the Forbidden City, the Ming Tombs, Tiananmen Square, and the Peking and Tsinghua Universities. I met hundreds of Chinese people and every evening had dinner with a different group of them. Many gave me gifts, took pictures and sang songs of greeting and appreciation. Even though our communication was limited, we were able to express our love for each other and the love God had for them. Throughout my stay I felt God's presence so strongly, and I know the people felt Him, too.

Before I returned home, the people gave me a Chinese name that means "the angel of love for the family." God placed that love in my heart in the sixth grade, before I really even knew Him, and He blessed me with the opportunity to express that love in person to the Chinese people in China. I will be forever grateful to God for that experience.

❀

When I looked over my collection of quilt patterns, I spied the name *East to Eden* and thought it was the perfect title for Sue's story. At first I was hesitant to use it because I could not find it anywhere on the internet, only on my typed list . . . and in all my frenzied typing, I could easily have keyed in the wrong name.

I checked with the American Quilter's Society to verify its existence, and was assured *East to Eden* is a bonafide nine-patch quilt block. Eight of the squares are pieced with two corner triangles opposite each other around a plain center square. The arrangement of the squares creates an arrow-like effect.

An arrow . . . pointing East, perhaps? I suppose it depends which way you place the quilt.

Sue's story affirms in my mind that the Lord created each of us with a purpose. Even if we walk away from Him, that purpose is still intact – just like what happened in Samson's life. Samson was born to deliver the Israelites from the Philistines. When he messed up with Delilah and was taken captive, it looked like God's purpose would not be fulfilled. But when Samson turned again to God and prayed, he destroyed a huge amount of Philistines – not just regular bad-guys, but leaders gathered to celebrate their victory over God's people.

I share Samson's story to make the point that even in the worst situation, God's purpose for our lives is woven into the very fiber of who we are. One of my favorite verses is "Faithful is he that calleth you, who also shall do it." (1 Thessalonians 5:24) If your hopes and dreams are from the Lord, He will make a way to accomplish them, just like he did for Sue as she traveled East to share Eden with the Chinese people she loved.

*A family is a
patchwork of love.*

~ 16 ~
Rainbow Cactus
Submitted by Alan Hahn of Waterford, Michigan

The midsummer's heavy thunderstorm turned the remote gravel road in rural northern Michigan into more of a hazard than any of us realized. We were caught completely off guard when we rounded a curve at about 35 miles per hour and our Pontiac Bonneville began to hydroplane out of control. Helplessly, my wife, two children, my mom and dad and I seemed to be floating as the car traveled sideways across the road headed toward a 10-foot drop off and an open field. The last thing I recall before putting my head between my legs was the large yellow sign indicating *curve in the road* – it was directly in line with my face in the passenger window as the vehicle hurtled on a collision course directly towards it.

The trip had been planned as a time of healing and recovery for my family – a time to reconnect after a devastating time in our lives. Only three weeks earlier, the first shock rocked our world. My wife of eight years and I had just put our five-year old son and three-year old daughter to bed for the night. We were relaxing in the evening and looking forward to an extended vacation in Michigan's Upper Peninsula when a call came at 10:00 p.m. that changed our plans.

My wife answered the phone. "Hi, Dad . . ." There was a pause as she attempted to understand my father's disturbing message. "What's wrong? What! Your son!?" She looked at me in state of shock and disbelief, and with a horrific look on her face she delivered the news with the phone hanging at her side, "Alan, your brother's dead!" I think I screamed "NO!" almost as if denying permission – it was a surreal moment.

My brother, my only sibling, 18 months my senior had moved to California – something he had talked about since any of us could remember. He left Michigan with a group of friends after his final year at Central Michigan University – just two days after he stood up as the best man in my wedding. He didn't have many prospects when he left for California, in fact the car he drove westward was coined the Asbird – a car that was half a Chevy Aster and half Pontiac Sunbird. For the first few years Glen struggled to find a job and generally find his way in life. But things seemed to finally work out and be going well for him. Only a few years ago we traveled there for his wedding, and I was honored to stand up as his best man. Glen was a husband and the father of a toddler son. His wife was expecting their second child, a daughter. He couldn't be gone now.

But it was true. Glen died at home in a matter of a few moments from a brain aneurism. One minute he was on the phone with his wife excited about tickets to the Angels' baseball game. The next moment he lay lifeless on the living room floor. By the grace of God, his wife knew something was wrong and came home. Their son was still tucked away in his crib when Mimi, three months pregnant, arrived home to find her husband dead. While the loss of my brother Glen was devastating, for his young wife it was a loss beyond words.

The trip to California for the funeral with several family members and friends was numbing – the entire trip a blur. An unending stream of tears ran down my face. One moment I would be fine, the next I sobbed uncontrollably.

And so my family tried to reconnect and console one another with a getaway to a friend's cabin "Up North." We visited former neighbors who retired a few years earlier and moved outside of Mackinaw City, Michigan. We enjoyed the afternoon visit with our friends as we laughed and cried remembering times with my brother. It was a relaxing day far removed from the noise of the city – "just what the doctor ordered."

But now this . . . this could not end well. If only we had slowed down. If only we would have let the roads dry a little while longer. If only. Though traveling 35 miles per hour, it was almost in slow motion that our car careened out of control heading towards the yellow metal sign and sign post. Were we going to flip and roll into the field or get pierced by the sign? In just moments so many thoughts can fill one's mind.

Within an instant the out of control car went from hydroplaning to a complete stop. We all looked around – was everyone ok? The children were crying, but we were all fine. I looked out my window. I didn't see the sign, but glancing down I saw the drop off – why weren't we falling?

The sign. It had stopped us from falling, acting as a fulcrum under the car.

I couldn't open the door, but I was able to climb out of the window. As I fell onto the wet foliage of the open field, I slipped down the embankment. "I don't see any damage to the car, but the undercarriage might be in bad shape," I reported. Moments later, a single car came down the road. "You all right?" the driver asked. "Yea, we're fine," I said. "Is there any chance I can get a ride to the Douglas'?"

While I was being taken back to our friend's house to arrange for a tow truck, the rest of the family waited in the car. My wife and mom held the kids who were still very upset. In an attempt to calm them, my wife said, "Kids, let's bow our heads and pray to God." It was just moments after they finished the prayer that my wife looked up in the eastern sky. . . and there it was; the symbol of God's promise so many years ago. The story was familiar even to my young children.

"Look Brandon and Britt, a rainbow. Remember God's promise to Noah? He is here and everything is going to be okay." My wife later told me that the rainbow not only instantly calmed our children, it soothed the adults' spirits as well.

Remarkably, there was no damage at all to the car. We pulled it out without incident and continued back to the cabin with no further problems. Seeing the rainbow that evening may have been overlooked by some as just another "natural phenomenon," a simple prism effect – light being separated into visible rays. But for my family it was indeed God speaking to us loud and clear, "I will never leave you or forsake you." It was a message we desperately needed at that moment that reaffirmed our faith.

Some words don't seem to fit together, like *rainbow* and *cactus;* however, there is a quilt pattern with this name that I felt related to Alan's touching message. His family experienced a devastating loss, topped by a dangerous car accident. The prickers of life were poking into this family causing great pain and discomfort.

But the Lord in His mercy didn't leave them without comfort. He reminded them of the great promises in His Word in a beautiful way even his young children could understand. The spiritual promises given in God's Word may seem unreachable, untouchable, so very far away . . . but they are real. Even when we face painful situations, our own personal "cactus," the Lord's promises are still sure, just as sure as the rainbow.

~ 17 ~
# King's Highway
Submitted by Evans Bissonette of Troy, Michigan

"How rich are you?"

I was taken off guard by the abruptness of my sister-in-law's statement and answered her with a puzzled look.

"Before he passed, your father told me he thought you were rich," she said. "You've kept it well hidden, so I figured the only way to find out was to ask. Just how rich are you?" The slight smirk playing at the corners of her mouth tempered her straightforward question, and I recognized the irony in her smile. It was one of those *I-laugh-so-as-not-to-cry* smiles.

Having just completed Dad's memorial service, maybe this bit of humor was the distraction we needed. I mulled over her words as she related the story Dad had told her.

Three years and three months earlier, almost to the day, Mom succumbed to cancer. By the grace of God, she had not suffered long. Dad was 88 at the time of her passing. His mind was still sharp, but a bum right arm and leg hampered his movements and limited his abilities to get around by himself. Before Mom's passing my parents supported each other, enabling them to maintain an independent lifestyle. Now, after over sixty years of marriage, she was gone. Dad tried to stay by himself in the house they had built together all those years ago, but a couple of falls shook him up enough to convince him that was not possible. We looked into assisted living and found a place in the country he liked then helped him make the move to his new residence.

Selling Dad's car, a vehicle he had babied since he drove it off the lot, was the last item to address. It was early spring when I drove the car from the old homestead to my brother's place. Dad rode along with me. On the way, I decided it would be a good idea to take the car through the car wash – get it cleaned up, waxed, and looking its best so anyone who came along would see it as the bargain it really was. As we exited the car wash, two young men armed with towels greeted us and busily wiped the water droplets off the exterior. I pulled a few bucks from my wallet and passed them over to dad in the passenger seat.

"What's this for?" Dad said looking over at me.

"It's a tip for the guys. Give it to them when they get done wiping the car."

"Didn't you pay the guy at the entrance? That should take care of it."

Preoccupied with the changes, those made and those yet to be made, I replied without much thought, "Probably. However those couple of dollars won't hurt me and, who knows, it may make a difference to them."

He sat silently as the guys finished up, then cracked the window and handed over the bills, then we drove off into the next phase of his life.

Time went by. I called a couple times a week and got up to see him as often as I could. He had always been a quiet man, never much for small talk, but over the few years before he passed he opened up and I got to learn a lot about my dad. He talked about his life. *I had an older brother, but he caught pneumonia when he was 12 and passed away.* He spoke of things he did when he was growing up on the family farm. *For the most part, it was a dairy farm, but we did have a few head of beef cattle, and horses to pull the equipment. No tractors, then . . .*

Dad talked about living through the Spanish flu pandemic; the Great Depression; two World Wars; rationing; learning to scrimp, to make do or do without. We covered many things. Some I had heard before; some not; but all interesting because he spoke of things we shared – our family history. Maybe he felt this was his last opportunity to pass along the torch.

"So, how rich are you?" The words echoed in my head.

Rich? In what ways can a person be rich? I don't have a lot of material things. Neither did Dad. In place of those, he preferred a belief in God and in life beyond the grave, in being kind and generous. For this, his reward here was a wife and children that loved him; food on the table; a roof over our heads; clothes on our backs; family and friends that were willing to gather around and celebrate both joyful and sad occasions; and the expectation of a greater reward in heaven. These were the riches he sought.

The important things I learned in life I learned from Dad. They were lessons passed on by someone who had experienced life and knew what mattered. Like my dad, I have a lot of things that really count – not material things, but the sort of things that make life rich. In that sense, he was right. I am rich. Very rich!

❀

I remember my first car. Purchased in 1983, my orange Datsun 1200 was ten years old with an am radio, no hubcaps, no air conditioning and 150,000 miles under its retreads. I was proud of that car, because I earned every penny of the $400 it cost, and she was mine, all mine.

I'm sure we all remember our first vehicles. I drive a nicer one now, and I'm thankful . . . especially when I put the key in and the ignition actually turns over. I remember a time in that old orange Datsun when I put the key in, and not only did it not start, but the key broke off in the ignition in the on position. Another car failed to continue running on the LBJ Freeway in Dallas. When I returned for it, broken glass and an oil slick told the tale of its fate.

I've been so exasperated by car problems I wrote a little praise chorus rejoicing that "There won't be any car repair, when we get over yonder." But what's more important than the car we drive is the path we are driving it on.

The vehicle we drive, as well as the things we accumulate on the road of life, do not reveal our greatest riches. Instead the *destination* tells the tale.

When we serve the Lord, we are truly traveling on the *King's Highway*, heaven bound. Serving God isn't always a smooth way, but it is the high way, the best way.

~ 18 ~
Whirlwind
Submitted by Lissa M. Lee of Madisonville, Louisiana

Last night I was invited to a friend's home for dinner. When I arrived, I was greeted by my friend and four new faces. None of us knew each other. Beth was our connection.

My friend Beth personifies the gift of hospitality. Everywhere she goes she strikes up conversations with total strangers, and before a person knows it, they have been invited to her home. A passionate Italian with deep Southern Louisiana roots, Beth and her husband Rod create meals so mouth-watering they make you want to "slap yo mamma," as the colloquialism goes.

Last night, however, Beth's friend Lynette prepared a salad of fresh greens, radishes, red onions and pecans all from her garden which she topped with homemade red wine vinaigrette. Laughter and onion breath filled the air as we munched the marvelous flavors at our equivalent to a guy's night of cards and cigars.

Conversations worked around the table, each of us introducing ourselves and relating our own "how we met Beth story." Within each distinctive story, a familiar thread of Beth's kindness wove each of us into her life.

The chatter sobered some when Susie, a displaced Chalmation from hurricane-ravaged New Orleans' Ninth Ward, related her story. She struggled for composure as she once again repeated the saga of the previous 18 months.

After Hurricane Katrina hit, most peoples' Ninth Ward reference point is the image broadcast immediately after the storm of thousands of families trapped in the Super Dome. That was only part of the picture. Another part was a thriving upper-middle-class community interconnected for almost a century.

In Chalmette, family homes passed from generation to generation lined block after block of the neighborhood. Mamères and pères (grandparents) built the first small homes. They lived in them until they outgrew them, then sold to a sibling and moved into a newer, larger home. As children grew up and married, they bought the starter houses, and the rest of the family moved up in a never-ending cycle. Multiply this process by decades, and you can see how the entire population of the little community is permanently linked together.

This was Susie's story. She moved into her mamère and père's home after she married. When she lost her husband, she faced new challenges, but with a strong support system, she knew her little family would be fine. Rather than put her son in a daycare facility, she built a business to support them. Her business thrived, and the time came for her to move. Twelve days before Hurricane Katrina hit, Susie left her grandparents' home and moved into her dream home.

On moving day, the entire street turned out to see her off. Everyone hugged and wept. This is unusual enough in today's society, but even more so when you consider Susie was only moving four blocks away. Chalmations share a matchless camaraderie.

Like so many other storms affecting the region, Katrina was just going to be a minor inconvenience to Susie. She packed, closed up her new house and headed off for a long weekend. Like everyone else, she believed she would be back in a few days, clean up her yard and wait for electricity to be restored – possibly throw out a few refrigerator items.

Her house was submerged for two weeks and drained over the next six. It was two months before she was allowed to see her home. Although Susie prepared with all the right insurance policies, her insurance only paid the contents portion of her policy. To collect flood insurance owners must have occupancy for a minimum of 30 days. All the hard work and responsible planning had been in vain; Susie was homeless, jobless and owed a $225,000 home loan.

But Susie was fortunate. Her parents cashed in her inheritance and paid off her bank loan. At 42 she faced starting over with absolutely nothing.

For the next six months, while she appraised her situation and made decisions, Susie and her son slept on friends' couches – a car, a few casual summer clothes, tennis shoes, sandals and toiletries the sum of all their possessions. Her mail was routed all over the country. Bills went unpaid. By Christmas her 800 credit rating was wiped out, and it was all she could do to wake up in the mornings. Grief and depression were doing their best to destroy her. If not for the responsibility of her son, she may have simply committed suicide like so many others.

Gradually the bills finally found her, and after months of negotiations with creditors some financial pressures resolved. She reopened her business in Northshore and now hopes to restore her clientele as word spreads to other displaced Chalmations of her return. Her son is in a good school, and they found a new home. Life is slowly moving forward.

As Susie spoke, I could tell she was still struggling. Although she is rebuilding her life, her reference point for all of life is still Chalmette. Like anyone dealing with a permanent loss, it is hard to accept that a treasured part of your life is forever a memory.

Beth has a tradition of closing her gatherings with prayer. Seated comfortably in the living room, sipping coffee, she asks if anyone has a specific need they would like prayer for. It is fun to watch people's reactions. Sometimes her visitors immediately voice concerns then suddenly regret their openness when they realize Beth means to pray right then. But Beth has a way about her that melts defenses. Though at first uncomfortable, guests relax in her genuine concern.

This night, instead of asking for requests, Beth told us we were going to pray for Susie. I could tell Susie was taken aback, but she welcomed the kindness. We sat quietly as Beth began praying for Susie's specific needs, and an indescribable warmth flooded the room. A sweet peace touched each one of us.

As I listened to Beth pray, I thought about how radically life changed for over 2 million people in one instant – how none of us are guaranteed anything in this life – and how easily we forget that. I thought about other times whole groups of people were displaced for a myriad of reasons. Throughout history people have been forced to flee their homes and rebuild in places they did not choose. We are not as unique as we sometimes think. We could learn much from the courageous examples of others.

As I prayed for Susie, I thought about all the displaced families I met through my job. At that moment, Susie sat in proxy for them all. Their faces flashed through my memory and I prayed for each one.

On the drive home I thought about how dramatically my own life changed over the past 18 months. Like Susie, I struggled with the emotions of facing new realities. I also thought about how changes in the natural relate to the changes Jesus brings into people's lives. In a sense, every believer is a "displaced person" – a native citizen of the Kingdom of Darkness divinely naturalized into the Kingdom of Life.

When a person becomes a Christian, things that never mattered before are suddenly important. What previously captured major attention, no longer holds any interest. New priorities are established with the realization that we are not our own. And just like any displaced person in the natural, it takes time for emotions to process these new spiritual realities. But, like Susie's situation, little by little, a new life begins to bloom.

Before leaving Beth's house, Susie told us a new family of Chalmations moved in across the street from her. She left us with a big smile and the parting words, "Dinner was simply divine!"

I'm a Kentucky girl converted to Michigander – a Yankee with the remnant of a Southern drawl for the last half of my life. Regarding natural disasters, Michigan's a relatively safe place – no tectonic plates shifting, no hurricanes blasting, not much flooding or forest fires, and no where near the amount of tornados as in other regions of the country. Although I have not personally faced a natural disaster of great magnitude, I recall with clarity the time a storm ripped through my world. I talk about this in detail in Chapter 42 "The Backing."

I described my situation this way. "It's like a tornado came and picked up the pieces of my happy life. They're spinning around me, and I don't know where they're going to land."

I'm not going to give away the ending. What I will do is issue this reminder: every situation we face is allowed in our lives by God. That's a tough pill to swallow. A lot of people have gagged on it. Sometimes life's trials are hotter than blazes and we see no good in them at all. Although never falsely imprisoned, persecuted or physically afflicted, I have faced my own fiery trials. In them I learned this: *God* is the good in them. Look to Him, not the situation.

Our hope is not in this world (in this world we *will* have tribulation). Our hope is in God. When the whirlwinds come, and they come to us all, remember that nothing can separate us from God or His love. No matter what we face, we face it with Jehovah-Jireh's promise of provision . . . and more than physical provision, He's promised wisdom. He's promised peace. He's promised guidance and direction. And when it's all said and done, He's promised Heaven..

Someone reading this is facing their own "ground zero" – building or rebuilding after a financial, emotional, physical, or spiritual storm. Have faith in God. And if you and I are thankfully not facing the monumental task of rebuilding in our lives, I pray the Lord gives us, as he gave Beth, the sensitivity to offer help to those who are.

Hem your blessings with thankfulness,
and they will not unravel.

~ 19 ~
Flower Basket
Submitted by Patty Cayten of Niles, Ohio

Gardening. I wish I had more time to enjoy the hobby, but I'm consumed with tilling, weeding, and planting of a different sort. Being mom to six daughters, my life is ever growing, never still.

We are a homeschool family, so I am very active in the education of my girls. Through the years I've come to realize that each family member is always in a perpetual stage of growth – from the youngest to the oldest, including myself and my husband.

The Bible says in Ecclesiastes 3 there is a time for every season. I believe this is true, but with my family sometimes I feel like I am in many seasons all at the same time. Some days, spring showers, summer sunshine, winter snow and fall dump all at the same time. It's like the weather in Michigan. You just don't know what to expect on any given day. And with so many girls, a bad hair day or hormones can set the world on its ear.

Beyond the daily activities, I've begun to see the stages of life we pass through as a type of planting cycle. My three teenage daughters are what I consider the beginning of a harvest. My husband and I have sown, watered, fertilized and protected them from the elements. Now we are beginning to see the results. It's a joy to discuss Scripture with them and see them grasping it as adults. They are making decisions according to their knowledge of the Word of God and their understanding of the consequences of breaching that Word. Of course, being human they stumble along the way, but their desire to live pleasing to the Lord is most important.

As every careful gardener knows, even grown plants need maintenance. Keeping that in mind, we are ever vigilant to guard against disease or insects that would inhibit our daughters from bearing fruit. A root of bitterness or destructive cankerworm could undo years of tending, even resulting in the death of a plant. So we keep our eyes and ears open and pray that God gives us the wisdom to deal with each child and each situation they face.

My two middle daughters are saplings, tender but somewhat established. We still provide a protective environment, but at the same time allow them guarded exposure to the elements they need to learn to live with. Some might call it giving them enough rope to hang themselves, but with purposeful training in mind we inch the doors open to allow interaction with the world and the opportunity for them to make their own decisions. We want them to see for themselves the consequences of seeking their own will over God's Word and realize that God's ways are best.

My husband and I diligently cover and fertilize these elementary-aged girls with the Word and lovingly prune and apply weed killer so they aren't overtaken with their own wills. Learning self control is a key to their future happiness.

My youngest is only a little sprout yet. Sally Anne is still in the greenhouse. We are very careful with her so she isn't damaged. She constantly reaches toward us for nutrients and support just as a sprout reaches upwards toward the sun, its source of nourishment and strength. We know that our little one is sown in good ground because she does indeed reach toward the "Son." She asks questions about God, and we have to be very careful of our answers. Our words fertilize her vulnerable spirit.

If a young plant receives fertilizer that is too concentrated, it will kill the plant. Right now our toddler just needs to know how much God loves her and that He is Creator of all things. We told her once how God hung the moon, stars and sun in the sky.

One evening a short time later, she gazed up at the moon and said in her shrill, three-year-old voice, "Look what that God did!"

And I say that with her. Look what that God did. He planted six souls in my garden, and my husband and I look forward to many years still tending and anticipating the harvests to come. We do so with much watchfulness, as a vineyardist tends the vineyard of Another, anticipating the return of the Owner with the desire of presenting Him with much fruit.

✂

When we are in the midst of raising children, it seems we will never have any time for ourselves again. From the moment that first little one comes home from the hospital, our priorities shift as we refocus on nurturing and caring for the person God brought into our lives through love.

Sometimes we have many children and events that overlap and bring seasons within seasons. We may be weeding in one field while we're seeding another, but by the grace of God, if we hang on, one day we will reap a beautiful harvest.

Mothers use many different methods to cultivate their children spiritually; they feed them the Word, prune and correct. They also sacrifice their own desires every day in ways their children don't realize. They give in small acts such as losing sleep to larger scale acts of giving like forfeiting a career, education, personal interest or hobby. I like to believe God makes a big compost pile out of all those personal desires left unplanted and sacrificed for our children. It may seem like a pile of disappointing rot, but really good fertilizer is made of waste products.

As I read Patty's story, I saw her in a field of flowers surrounded by colorful blossoms. The beauty and fragrance brought a satisfied smile to her sweet freckled face as she carried a woven basket over her arm and collected flowers in the sunshine. Because she is my friend, I know she has gone through many trials and sown in tears, but I believe with all my heart that she will reap with joy. So if you are sowing in tears or have a pile of unrealized dreams that seems to have gone to waste, I hope the Lord will give you the vision to see the fruit from your fertilizer and you will collect your own beautiful basket of flowers in the Son-shine.

~ 20 ~
Joy Bells
Submitted by Irvin L. Rozier of Blackshear, Georgia

The Lord blessed me with two wonderful daughters and a fine son. In 1986, when the children were 6, 8, and 11, my wife left us and I became a single parent. The children missed their mother terribly, and my heart grieved for them. But through the tragedy, the Lord reached into my broken heart and saved me.

After I became a Christian, I began praying for my children. In December 1989, I prayed they would be blessed with a wonderful Christmas. I specifically asked for some time with their mother. I shouldn't have been surprised when she called a short time later and asked if they could visit over the holidays. I readily agreed.

The children were excited. Since our separation, visits with their mother had been rare. She lived in Atlanta, so we set a meeting place at a halfway point in Dublin. After packing and scraping together a few dollars for the trip, we loaded up the car and headed out.

Before my wife left, she had been a loving, nurturing mother, always making sure the children were well fed, clothed, cleaned, hugged and loved. She roller-skated with them and read to them – they were her life. Tragically, even a mother's concern for her children is vulnerable to satan's deceptions – by drug use or other methods – and my wife's bond with her family deteriorated, ultimately taking her far away from us.

The high spirits in the car escalated with the passing of each mile. We finally arrived with wiggles and giggles, and I wish you could have seen the joy on their faces as the children hugged and greeted their mother. We exchanged good-byes, then the children climbed in their mother's car and drove away. I sat in my car and cried – tears of joy for their happiness and tears of grief for their losses.

Preparing myself for the journey home, I stared at my car's fuel gauge which indicated the gas tank was almost empty. I was 110 miles from home and had no money to buy gas. But what could I do? I began driving back and prayed, "Lord, I guess I'll run out of gas within a few miles, but I'm trusting You in this situation."

About three miles down the road, I saw a sign pointing to a small country church. The Lord spoke to me and said, "Go to that church."

It was 10:30 a.m. on a Sunday morning. "Okay," I said, "but I'm not dressed very well."

The Lord replied, "Go just like you are and don't even concern yourself about what others may think about your clothing. I know what is in your heart."

I drove up to the church, got out of my beat up old Toyota and went inside. Service had started and several heads turned to stare as I entered. After a few songs, the preacher spoke on the famous faith chapter, Hebrews 11.

The Lord anointed the pastor. It seemed the words he spoke were directed right at me, and I needed encouragement at that particular moment. At the conclusion of the service, the preacher asked for testimonies. The stories of those that testified were very uplifting.

Sitting, listening, relaxing, the Lord startled me when He said, "Irvin, get up and testify."

I stood, wiped some of the wrinkles from my blue jeans and began to speak. Every eye in the congregation was on me and every ear attentive to my words. I told the people how the Lord directed me to their church, how the sermon and testimonies encouraged me, and how happy I was that my children could spend a few days with their mother. Then I asked for prayer. The godly pastor instructed his little flock to gather around the altar and pray that not only my children, but other children from broken homes would have a happy Christmas.

Afterwards, I slowly walked to my Toyota. I was almost there when an elderly woman approached, shook my hand, and told me my testimony touched her heart. When I withdrew my hand, a five dollar bill rested in my palm. Gas money to get home! God provided when I obeyed His voice.

When I arrived home that Sunday evening, a friend called and asked me to drive him to a job about 50 miles away. A nurse who was going to work two 16-hour shifts over Christmas, my friend planned to rent a hotel room where I could stay while he worked. With my children away, I was free to go.

It snowed hard the night before we left. But snow wasn't the worst of it – the temperature dropped, and dangerous black ice formed on the roadways. Along the way we saw many vehicles stuck in ditches. In South Georgia, people are not equipped to drive in icy conditions, and as I applied my brakes at an intersection, I hit a patch of black ice.

"Brace yourself, we're going to crash," I warned. Sure enough, we did. Thankfully, the Lord protected us both from injury and the car received only a small dent. It was, however, stuck in the ditch. We set out on foot searching for help and met a kindhearted farmer who immediately pulled on his brogans, walked into his shed, cranked up his John Deere, and pulled us out of the ditch. We tried to pay him, but he refused. Thank God for people like this benevolent farmer.

We arrived safely at the hotel, checked in, and went out for a bite to eat. Afterwards, I drove my friend to the nursing home and returned to the hotel to sleep. The next morning, Christmas Eve, I woke up early and said, "Lord, I sure would like to go to church this morning. Show me where to go." Looking over the newspaper, I located a church conducting an early morning service.

"Go there," the Lord said. So I went, and although only 30-something people attended, the service was sweet and the words spoken about our Savior's birth blessed me.

"Lord, I sure would like to go to Sunday school," I prayed when service was over. "Please show me where to go."

He led me out of town and into a beautiful country with gently rolling, snow-covered hills sparkling in the sunshine. As I was driving, I thought about Christmas. My friend planned to pay me $50 for driving him to his job. Although I was thankful for it, it was not much to buy Christmas for three children.

While I was meandering and musing, the Lord interrupted my thoughts with a command, "Turn left here on this dirt road." I did and after about two miles I came to a quaint little church sitting on a hill. "Here is where I want you to go for Sunday school."

I felt a warm, peaceful presence as I entered the parking lot. Friendly people greeted me and directed me to the right room. *These people are genuine,* I thought to myself. *This is a praying church that God loves.*

The Lord directed me to leave after Sunday school, so I returned to the hotel, had a bite to eat and took a nap – until 2:30 p.m. The Lord woke me with the words, "Go on over to the nursing home." I obeyed.

I found my friend and while we were talking, I heard singing in another room. "I'm going down there to listen," I told him and followed the sound of music. When I entered the room, I recognized many of the folks conducting the service from the country church I visited that morning. They remembered me and invited me to join them, which I did, thoroughly enjoying the carols and old hymns in the presence of the Lord.

After service, I said my good-byes and walked down the hall to the nurses' station looking for my friend. The preacher caught up with me there and said, "The Lord told me to give you this check." It was $150.

I had asked the Lord for money to buy my children gifts for Christmas. He tested my faith, ordering my steps, and I thank

God I listened and obeyed. I drove my friend home and my children returned late Christmas Day. We commemorated the birth of our Lord together with a simple Christmas celebration. I was so glad to see them and thankful for all God provided to make our holiday special. God answers prayer.

❇

Irvin's narrative inspires me to listen more closely for the voice of the Lord in my life – and then to follow His direction. I love a story with a happy ending and I thank Irvin for sharing his with us. Certainly many more challenges faced this single father as he raised his children, but with God, he and we can do all things.

The Christmas theme of Irvin's story inspired me to title it after the quilt pattern *Joy Bells*. The more I thought about it, the more I liked it. The visual of Christmas bells trimmed in holly and red ribbon brings cheery thoughts of holiday celebrations. The peal of Christmas greeting as clapper connects with cast metal draws my attention from things seen to things heard, then ultimately to a response.

Most bells ring for reaction. Doorbells, telephones and fire alarms all evoke responses from their hearers. "Answer me!" "Talk to me!" "Get out of the way!" I pray that you and I will hear the resounding cries of God's alarms as well as the still quiet voice that directs our paths, and may we have joy in the ringing and the seasons.

Friendship is like a patchwork quilt of caring words,
thoughtful deeds, and lots of laughter,
all stitched together with understanding.

~ 21 ~
Capital T
Submitted by John Wood of Las Vegas, Nevada

For years I lived in that dark place called addiction, a place filled with fear and loneliness that only the addicted person can know. One day I found myself standing at the edge of the abyss. All hope gone I was on the verge of taking the last fatal step. But, a man named Bill put his hand on my shoulder and said, "I see your pain. Let's talk."

Actually, Bill did the talking. He told me about himself, how he too had fought with his addiction to alcohol for more years than I'd been alive. As I listened, I heard my story. At first I thought sure he had been reading my mail. But, Bill was happy. He laughed as he told his story, and there was joy in the telling. His willingness to share changed my life forever.

He told it simply, about what it had been like, what had happened and what it was like now. But when Bill finished, I wanted what he had. I wanted it enough not to take that last fatal step. We talked late into the night sharing our lives and for the first time I met someone who knew my fears, who had looked into the abyss. I would find that he knew me better than I knew myself.

With Bill's support I stayed sober for six months. At first I rejoiced at my apparent wellness, but it was short lived. It's called "white knuckle sobriety." I was sober, but I still had the fear of drinking. It was a fear that tormented me even in my dreams.

One day Bill asked me, "Have you ever asked God for help?"

"I don't believe in that, Bill."

"John, let me share something with you. I was given this by a friend early in my sobriety, it helped me. Maybe it'll help you."

Bill rummaged around on his desk and found a book. He opened it to the last page and handed it to me. This is what I read:

"There is a principle which is a bar against all information, which is proof against all arguments and which cannot fail to keep a man in everlasting ignorance – that principle is contempt prior to investigation." - Herbert Spencer

"John, try it. When you go home tonight, humble yourself, kneel, ask Him to remove the compulsion."

"But what do I say? I've never prayed before."

"Prayer is nothing more than you talking to God. You talk, He'll listen. It's not complicated."

That night in my room my embarrassment nearly held me back. But my fear of drinking drove me to my knees. There in the dark I finally let go. Out loud I begged God. "Please take this away!" Nothing happened. There was no flash of light there was no voice from above. Disappointed, I crawled into bed and slept.

It wasn't until several days later that a friend at work asked, "What's up with you? I've never seen you so happy."

It was then I realized that I didn't need or even want a drink. I realized that it had been days since I'd even thought of drinking! God had removed the desire to drink.

That wasn't the end of it, of course. I had a lot to learn and a lot to do. I still had a great deal of shame to deal with, and there were all those people I'd harmed along the way. I would need to clean house and get my life in order. There could be no excuses for me to pick up a drink. I had to clear away the wreckage of my past.

One weekend I went to a retreat. A bunch of alcoholics had come together to share. I had been sober for a while but something still nagged at me – something that threatened to give me the excuse to drink again. I heard a woman talk about her life, about having been abused when she was just a girl. She spoke without fear or shame of her past. My mind began to race, for she talked of the very thing I could not talk about. When she finished I went looking for another alcoholic to talk to.

His name was Ralph; he had been in the French Foreign Legion and was now a priest. I asked if we could talk and he agreed. I told him about the abuse and my shame and when I finished he asked, "That's it? That's what you've been afraid of?"

"Yes," I confessed, "I have been afraid someone would find out."

"John, let go. Your fear has made it bigger than it is. Here give me your hand."

He took my hand in his and gently slapped the back of it. "There, you have been punished enough. You have shared once, and now you will have no fear to share again."

On the way home that night I stopped at a friend's home. There was a young man visiting him who was having trouble with his sobriety. He told a story of abuse when he was young, and his shame.

I said, "You know, that happened to me also. I was abused. There are lots of us this has happened to. You don't have to be ashamed." It was then I realized God had turned my shame into a tool of recovery.

A year later I received a call late one night. It was the young man. "John, I'm sober one year today. Thanks."

It's been 27 years since I met Bill and God, and I'm still clean and sober. As Mr. Herbert Spencer suggested, I've tried to keep an open mind. But Bill taught me one more thing – to keep it, I have to give it away. When someone stands at the abyss, I'm ready and willing through the grace of God, to share. In so doing, I save my own life for one more day and offer hope to others in need.

�֎

The *Capital T* quilt pattern is a symbol for temperance. Although I believe John's addiction to alcohol went far beyond a lack of self control, the symbolism lead me to select this design for his story.

The 18th amendment to the U.S. Constitution banned the legal use of alcohol in 1919. Only 24 years later, the amendment was repealed and "evil drink" flowed freely once again.

I'm not a psychologist or a politician, but I believe prohibition failed because by its very name, temperance means moderation or self-restraint. The sale of liquor or "spirits" thrives because men seek to fill the void – escape from the realities of life. Apart from God, men find this in alcohol and other mind-altering substances, and once hooked, moderation and self-restraint are almost impossible to muster – without God.

Capital T is for Truth – the Spirit of Truth that delivers people from the gods of addiction that control and cost so much to those who serve them. But when you know Him, you know everything you need to live free from addiction's bonds.

And ye shall know the truth, and the truth shall make you free. (John 8:32)

Jesus said to him, 'I am the way, the truth, and the life . . . (John 14:6)

~ 22 ~
Crown of Thorns
Submitted by Rachel Lowrence of Southfield, Michigan

I took my tennis racket out and began to warm up. It was a humid June day and tournament day for my tennis class. The week before, I lost a long set to Chanelle, and I was in second place. Charity, her sister, was in third place.

All through the session the kids in the class had been earning points by playing sets against each other. Because Chanelle had gotten the most points throughout the session, she already attained the league championship. But today I had a chance to get the tournament trophy if I won my set playing against her.

First I had to play Charity. I felt confident I could win against her. The set was lengthy, and I played hard. Hot and tired, I wondered how I would be able to play another set, and against the league champion. In the end I won over Charity with a score of six to four. When the game was over, Charity and I met at the net and we shook hands.

"Good game," she said. I could tell she was upset about losing and struggled to conceal her feelings.

"Good game," I said. "You did really well."

"Thanks," she said.

I sat on a picnic table bench and sighed. My heart rate was rapid and my tongue stuck to the roof of my mouth. I gulped down water and prepared myself to face Chanelle. I knew I would be exhausted when I was done, but still, this was my chance.

I served to start the set. I was surprised how well I was able to serve – at least I hit the ball in most of the time and I was able to aim. We were well matched (even though I had already played a tiring set), and we battled for each point a long time.

The game dragged on. At one point we heard thunder, and the sky grew overcast, but thankfully it didn't rain. Most of the players had finished their sets and left, but Chanelle and I continued on. With a score of four to four, I was so tired I could hardly see straight, much less hit the ball.

I forced myself to keep playing. After a while I started feeling I would never win the game, but I realized that as long as I focused only on hitting the ball, and not on how many games I had won or lost, I was able to keep going. Every time I thought *You're going to lose, Rachel, you're going to lose!* I would say to myself: *No, keep trying!* And so, I was able to persevere.

Finally, Coach Randy called over to check the score. It was six to six, so the coach called for a tie-breaker. We had played at least a half hour after the time class usually ended.

On one hand, I was relieved the game was finally going to end. At the same time, I was a bit upset because I felt my chances for a win decreased, since I play better over a long period of time.

A tie-breaker is one game that goes to seven points. You don't have to win by two either, so when it was six to six, I was really nervous. I had a sudden fleeting vision of Chanelle with the trophy, but I shook it off. Everyone was watching us as we each ran around the court, doggedly hitting the ball back and forth. Finally, I hit the ball too far.

"Out!" cried Chanelle, but surprisingly, her voice was not as much triumphant as it was relieved.

I sighed, and tried to swallow my disappointment. I had wanted so much to win. *Would I ever be able to beat Chanelle?* I asked myself.

Chanelle and I met at the net and shook hands.

"G-good game." I said, trying not to let my voice show I was near tears.

"You played really well," Chanelle said.

"You did, too." I attempted a smile.

The coach called us to the award table where he presented Chanelle the first-place trophy for the tournament as well as a trophy for the league championship. Then he turned to me.

"I'd like to give Rachel the good sportsmanship award," he said. "She's always kept her cool and never blown it."

I was so amazed that I had to smile. I took the trophy from my coach, and Mom took a picture of me with it. It was almost as if my teacher had planned it this way so I would feel better after I lost. *God, you knew what was going to happen,* I thought to myself. The trophy and recognition were a comfort, and the Lord taught me a great lesson through the whole ordeal.

I realized that winning the tournament wasn't everything. I mean, I might have beaten Chanelle if I hadn't played Charity first, and Chanelle just as easily could have gotten the good sportsmanship award, because she really was a good sport.

As I thought back over the game, I realized how friendly it was, even though we were competing against each other. We each praised each other's good plays, and often we argued for the other person's benefit.

When we were about to leave, I asked Chanelle for her number so we could get together and play more over the summer. I didn't have any hard feelings about that game, and I'm actually thankful I didn't win. Because I lost, I learned how to be a good sport. And a good sport doesn't care if they win or lose.

❋

Nobody wants to lose. And if we have to lose, why do we have to be good sports about it, anyway? Like losing isn't bad enough? Is good sportsmanship even in the Bible?

Well, the Word does say to do everything without complaining – and to rejoice with those who rejoice.

The message of Rachel's story transcends the tennis court. She lost a prize she wanted and worked diligently for, but in the end received an award for something far greater than scoring more points than her opponent. The award she received recognized her character – character gained through learning to accept painful loss, and that is why I titled her story with the quilt pattern *Crown of Thorns.*

Our Lord received His crown of thorns on the way to the His death on the cross. To those around Him, it looked like a great defeat, but the temporary suffering resulted in an eternal victory for Him and for His church.

And on a two-for-one bonus, this story reminded me of another lesson – one about Christians who become competitive when their focus is on self – wanting that solo, or to be the head teacher of that class, or the department leader of that ministry.

When a brother or sister in Christ achieves something we desire for ourselves, we should rejoice with them. God knows what He's doing, and He's working things out in the lives of all concerned according to His purpose.

If a thorn pokes your flesh, don't leave it there and allow infection to set in. Pull it out. Clean the wound. Be healed. And in all things give thanks. We're working for the Kingdom of God, not the kingdom of self. That is why we rejoice with those who rejoice, even when we face a personal disappointment. In the process, we develop godly character that will outshine any jewel-studded golden crown or trophy.

~ 23 ~
Garden Walk
Submitted by Margie Stoller of Bloomfield Hills, Michigan

Sometimes it is only in retrospect we see God working in our lives. When we go through difficult situations, it is easy to forget to look for the signs that He is near – or to cry out to Him for help. At least that is what happened to me. I forgot to turn to Him when I faced the most difficult situation of my life and tried to handle it on my own.

We didn't realize it, but my mom, in her 80s at the time, was experiencing the beginning stages of dementia. I was living in Colorado with my husband and two children, and Mom was living in Florida, so we weren't able to visit as often as we would have liked. We spoke on the phone several times a week sharing the details of our lives and trying to bridge the gap the distance created. Whenever we talked Mom always reassured me she was "doing fine," though I knew the stress of seeing my sister living in a nursing home while disabled from a series of brain tumors made life difficult for her.

Our mom was a very independent and strong woman who trusted that the Lord would never give her more than she could handle and who turned to Him in song to help her through her difficult days. Knowing that, I felt comfortable leaving her to continue life on her own – at least for a few more years.

Mom certainly surprised us when she broke the news she had met a wonderful man and they were going to marry. He told her he didn't want to waste any time since they were "not getting any younger." He wanted to get married right away.

119

We didn't realize what was happening. We were pleased mom found a friend and a companion and that she was happy. At the same time, we advised her against rushing into marriage. But Mom was an independent woman who made her own decisions, and she assured us that everything would be okay. Despite our advice, she got married less than four months after meeting this man.

In the years that followed, a living nightmare unfolded. I felt strongly that Mom, because of her dementia, was being taken advantage of emotionally, psychologically, medically and financially. I yearned to help her but was told the law protected her new husband's rights to determine her care. I had no say, I could not intervene, and it broke my heart.

I was convinced my precious mother was being mistreated and was suffering. I had promised her long ago I would be there when she needed me, but my hands were tied, and I could not help. No one believed me. I spent days on the phone trying to find assistance from a Florida resource. Certainly, I thought the social service or senior citizen agencies would be concerned. But no one wanted to get involved. No one offered to support or help me. I was "only a daughter," and the law said I did not have the power to make any decisions for her.

I cried until I had no more tears. I spent days in bed depressed and angry at God for not helping my mom. I stopped praying, then I turned away from the Lord.

It wasn't until *after* Mom's death that the Lord showed me He had been with me all along – even when I doubted and turned from Him in my dismay.

Weeks before she passed, I made travel arrangements to visit Mom in Florida. Of course, when I scheduled the trip I had no way of knowing she was about to make a turn for the worst. Two days before my husband and I arrived in Florida, her health began deteriorating. Although it wasn't the visit I had hoped for, the Lord provided this opportunity for me to sit by Mom's side, hold her hand and sing to her during the last two days of her life. I thank God for ordering my steps and divinely orchestrating schedules to give me the chance to be with Mom and reassure her of my love before He called her home. Looking back, I realize the timing was perfect.

Since the song "Because You Loved Me" expressed my feelings for Mom in such a beautiful way, I sent her the lyrics several months before she passed. During the planning of her memorial, I mentioned to my sister-in-law that I wished I had the CD with me so we could play the song during the service. My nephew was standing nearby, overheard me and said, "Aunt Margie, you won't believe this, but this morning as we were leaving, I went back into the house to get that CD. I didn't know why, but I just wanted to bring it with me."

Mom . . .

> *You were my strength when I was weak*
> *You were my voice when I couldn't speak*
> *You were my eyes when I couldn't see*
> *You saw the best there was in me*
> *Lifted me up when I couldn't reach*
> *You gave me faith 'cause you believed*
> *I'm everything I am*
> *Because you loved me*

Knowing the song that conveyed my deep feelings of love and gratitude for my mother would be played at the service brought another level of peace to my heart. God had provided again.

And, just in case I wasn't getting the message the Lord was trying to send me, as I entered the room to see Mom in her casket for the first time, I stood in amazement as the song "In the Garden" played through the funeral home's music system. Any reservations I had about God melted as the familiar words washed over my spirit.

I come to the garden alone
While the dew is still on the roses
And the voice I hear, falling on my ear
The Son of God discloses

And He walks with me
And He talks with me
And He tells me I am His own
And the joy we share as we tarry there
None other has ever known

"OK, Lord, I get it," I said loudly enough for anyone nearby to hear. I finally got the message He'd been trying to get through to me.

Every summer – every single summer during my years at home, Mom, my sister and I sang that song in our church. It was our song – our special trio. I hadn't told anyone; nor had I requested the song be played. I am convinced the Lord used it to reassure me that He was with me – that He had indeed been with me throughout my long ordeal. He was waiting to be my resource. If only I had trusted Him and turned to Him; perhaps, I could have prevented some of those tears.

I've learned my lesson, and when my days are bright or especially when they are difficult, I know without a doubt that my Lord is with me. And, sometimes on those difficult days, I find myself turning to the Lord in song, just as Mom always did, and take a walk in the garden with the One who calls me His own.

✻

I believe God has a special affinity for gardens. He started His relationship with mankind in a garden. He walked with Adam and Eve in Eden in the cool of the day.

Jesus spent a difficult night in a garden outside Jerusalem. After the Last Supper, he retired to Gethsemane where he sweat blood as He agonized over the weight of sin He was about to carry to the cross. In the same garden, He was betrayed by the kiss of a "friend" and abandoned by those closest to Him.

And from a garden tomb, Jesus Christ resurrected from the dead, bringing hope and new life to all that believe.

I titled Margie's story with the quilt pattern *Garden Walk*. As I read her account, I saw Margie transition through several "gardens" in her life. At her mother's side, as a young person she sang about a lovely garden meeting place with the Lord – a song of intimacy and relationship with God. As the years passed and her mother aged, Margie agonized in her personal Gethsemane with feelings of betrayal and abandonment. But the story doesn't end in Gethsemane's garden. God made sure Margie got the message that He was there, even when she didn't recognize His presence – like Mary Magdalene beside the garden tomb after the resurrection of Jesus.

Charles Austin Miles wrote the song "In the Garden" in 1913 after reading the account of Mary Magdalene's approach to the sepulcher the Sunday morning of Jesus' resurrection. It was very early in the morning, and Mary was in agony of soul as she sought the missing body of Christ. But the Lord spoke her name, "Mary," and His voice blotted out everything else – from the sweet singing of birds to the heartache of loss. Jesus Christ is the God of all our gardens, and regardless of the path we are on, we are on a "Garden Walk" with Him.

Good friends are like quilts:
they age with you,
yet never lose their warmth.

~ 24 ~
Britches
Submitted by Brad Paulson of Spokane, Washington

To improve is to change; to be perfect is to change often.

Winston Churchill was not referring to parenting when he uttered these words; however, if he had been, I would have gone right out and bought his parenting book. My greatest achievements, as well as my greatest failures in life, have all revolved around fatherhood and my ability to adapt to change. In the infancy of my venture into parenting I realized that great triumphs and failures could be experienced in one short visit to the changing table.

Like many men, I was not fully prepared for the degree of servanthood required by new daddies. My wife seemed to step into her mommy role with such ease it seemed she had been training for it all her life. While I spent my formative years playing with trucks and shooting army men with rubber bands, she cared for her dolls and made sure the cat was dressed up nice. I approached fatherhood knowing it would require some sacrifice, but I didn't realize the severity of my underestimation until my early attempts at diaper changing.

My wife and I spent many hours setting up the nursery. I restored the crib my parents had used for my sister and me, we wallpapered and decorated in primary colors, and I even crafted a solid oak cradle. It all seemed pleasant and good, except for the vinyl clad mystery that loomed in the corner – the changing table. My wife convinced me we should get one, but I did not see the need for it.

125

"Why can't we just change him in the crib?" I asked innocently. My wife responded with a chuckle and the "you've got to be kidding" look. The table had some compartments for stuff; I figured we'd keep some toys and maybe a blanket in them. The top was a padded flat surface, but it was vinyl and didn't look very comfortable. Surely our newborn would prefer having his diaper changed in the comfort of my lap.

At last, the glorious day of my son's birth arrived. I had dreamed of it for years, but never did I imagine how tired I would be. I knew that women always seemed to go into labor in the middle of the night, but I was unaware that it was usually another twenty-four hours before they actually gave birth. My fear had been that I might miss breakfast; I never expected to miss a whole day.

After the delivery, about the time things finally quieted down and I was able to fall asleep in the most uncomfortable chair in the hospital, our relatives began streaming in. Hours passed until the last visitor bid farewell. Then the hospital kicked us out. I couldn't believe they were sending me out in my delicate condition, and my wife seemed tired, too. The thought of stretching out in my own bed did seem appealing, so I didn't put up a fuss.

Arriving home, my wife informed me that she needed to sleep and that I needed to care for the baby. It seemed odd that she was the tired one (she had been lying down most of the time at the hospital while I had been standing), but I figured my son and I could bond with a little nap on the loveseat in the nursery. My wife retired to our bedroom, and I got comfortable on the loveseat holding my son close to my heart.

It was a precious moment that lasted nearly seven minutes. Then a strange sound filled the room followed by an even stranger warm sensation on my shirt and arms. Our new parents class never covered diaper leakage – the grim reality now staring me in the face. Then, out of the corner of my eye, I spied the changing table, and a sense of hope filled my heart.

I rushed over to the table. Being as gentle with my child as I could, I placed him on it and then frantically removed my shirt, threw it in the garbage and began to scrub myself with baby wipes. A cry brought me back to a state of consciousness. I looked down at my son, completely helpless and in great need of a few diaper wipes himself. I had never changed a diaper alone before, but how hard could it be?

The first challenge was to remove the old diaper without touching it – further complicated by the jerky little movements of my son's legs. I managed to undo the adhesive tapes and open up the diaper. I stepped back in shock at the sight of it . . . and the realization that I wasn't wearing protective gloves or safety goggles. It was at that moment those chubby little legs kicked in to high gear stomping in the mess I was trying to clean up. In one smooth, fluid motion, I snatched the dirty diaper, tossed it into the pail and grabbed a clean one. I thought the nightmare was almost over, until I realized he was dirtying another diaper, and the new one hadn't even been installed yet. It was becoming apparent why my wife insisted on buying the changing table. The thought of trying to do this on my lap sent shivers down my spine.

Needless to say, we survived that ordeal. My wife even managed to sleep through it. Many new discoveries followed, centered around that changing table. I learned that just when you think you've got everything under control, God seems to throw you a curve ball, like introducing solid food. I also learned practical lessons, like covering a baby boy's privates with a diaper rag when changing; it's not just for modesty's sake.

The greatest thing I learned was that I had someone who needed me. No matter how big a mess he made, I would be there to clean him up. There were times when a major diaper eruption brought on the feeling that he would never be clean again, that he was ruined. As a loving father I had to approach those moments with care, diligence and sometimes several packages of diaper wipes. No mess was ever too big, and no cleanup operation, even though some took longer than others, ever failed to provide the desired results.

That baby boy is almost sixteen years old now. Through the years we have taught each other many things. Currently I am teaching him how to drive, and he is teaching me that, during some of the near-misses we have had, it might be beneficial if I wore diapers.

If I had to choose the single most important thing fatherhood has taught me, it would be that having someone who needs you is a beautiful thing. I realize that God must delight in my dependency on him. During the times He has helped me clean up the messes I have made in my life, He never stopped loving me. Change is inevitable, and with each change comes a new kind of mess, but the love of the Father never fails to make right what we have made wrong. And with each change comes a renewed strength to move on to the next challenge.

�֎

Brad originally titled his story, "A Change for the Better" – a fitting headline, indeed. But in keeping with the quilt theme of this project, I couldn't resist titling his story after the pattern *Britches*.

I called my youngest "Little Britches," then "Little Britches Wagner," then just "LBW" as she scampered, ruffle-covered-diaper-in-air, across the carpet on all fours. With four kids, the Wagner household certainly experienced some of our own diaper dramas . . . and the fun didn't stop there. Colds, flues and other conditions issued forth their own fountains of bodily emissions to be cleaned. After all the wiping, laundering and sanitizing, the adorable little person looking at me with loving, trusting eyes was worth the leaks, squeaks and squishes.

Thank you, Brad, for sharing your story and your humor . . . and reminding us that we are all dependant upon the Lord who helps us through life's "changes" and "messes" with unfailing love. With God as our Father, we can't get "too big for our britches."

~ 25 ~
Dove in the Window
Submitted by Dixie Phillips of Floyd, Iowa

My husband and I were overjoyed at the birth of our second child. John Drake Phillips weighed in at 8 pounds 10 ounces and was born with a black eye – our "heavyweight fighter" we joked. Ironically, in just a few days our little champion faced a fight for his very life.

Baby John awoke the morning of his two-week birthday in distress. He was whimpering like a sick puppy, so I went to his crib to see what was wrong. I couldn't get him to open his eyes.

Picking him up, I tried to get him to nurse, without success. The entire time his eyes were tightly closed and he continued his high-pitched whine. I rushed him to the doctor's office where I was advised go immediately to the hospital. My baby was admitted. My husband and I were in shock. What happened? How did our healthy son get so sick?

After several tests, a pediatrician met with us. He was very somber as he gave the diagnosis: bacterial spinal meningitis. John could die.

The doctor said John probably picked up a bug in the delivery room that over the previous two weeks infiltrated his entire system. Our hearts beat wildly. It felt like we were in the middle of a bad dream. The doctor went on to explain that if John's fever broke, he might have a chance.

Over the next twelve days, my husband and I took turns spending the night at the hospital. Our two-year-old daughter didn't understand why she had to be separated from us, and we tried to keep life as normal as possible for her.

129

For days the fever continued to rage in John's limp body. The evening of the seventh day I stood by his bed and whispered in his little ear, "Don't give up, baby. Don't give up." My spirit cried out to his, "Keep fighting, John. Your daddy and mommy love you so much."

I was not allowed to hold my baby, so I pumped breast milk in hopes that he would eat it. As I sat in the hospital room, a nurse turned the television to *The 700 Club*. A gospel group was singing a song.

> *How sweet to hold a newborn baby.*
> *And feel the pride and joy he gives.*
> *But greater still the calm assurance,*
> *This child can face uncertain days,*
> *Because He lives.*
> *Because He lives I can face tomorrow.*
> *Because He lives all fear is gone.*
> *Because I know He holds the future,*
> *And life is worth the living just because He lives.*

I can't explain what happened during that song, but I started crying uncontrollably. I knew I was no longer alone in that hopeless place. The Presence of God had come into the room. As if the musicians were physically in the room with me, one of the singers stopped the song and said she had a Word from the Lord for some young mother watching the program.

"There's a newborn baby boy who is very sick in the hospital," she said.

I sat there stunned as she continued, "The walls of the hospital room are green."

I looked at the hospital walls. They were green. I couldn't believe my ears. She went on to describe how the crib was under a window – exactly like John's crib.

"The doctors told you that your little boy might not live, but God wants you to know that this sickness is not unto death. Your baby is going to live."

The group went on to finish the song. As they sang the final chorus, a peace swept over me, and I knew John was going to live. I knew God was going to heal my little boy.

I crossed the room to his crib and felt his forehead. He still had a high fever, but I raised my hands to Heaven anyway and began to thank God for healing my son. I knew I was standing on holy ground and that God was granting a miracle to my family. In the middle of the night John's fever broke.

"John has had a high fever several days," the doctor said the next morning. "He is going to live, but he might have brain damage."

Amazingly, my heart stayed peaceful at the announcement. No fear, no "what ifs" terrorized my soul. I had experienced a visit from Heaven, and I knew that John was healed. Five days later we took our baby boy home completely whole.

Twenty six years have passed, and we still reminisce about the day Jesus visited our baby in that green hospital room and healed him. We are convinced that without God's supernatural touch from Heaven, our little boy wouldn't have had a fighting chance – even though he was born with a black eye.

Dixie's story brought to mind the *Dove in the Window* quilt pattern – a block that, ironically, looks more like a cross than a dove.

As I read the details surrounding baby John's illness, I imagined the television screen in the hospital room as a window God used to bring a message of peace to Dixie's worried heart. God still works miracles, and I praise Him for raising up her son.

Dixie's story touched me with a personal memory. When my first husband was fighting cancer, I took a leave from platform ministry. After he passed, the first song I sang was the same Gaither song that touched Dixie and has impacted so many lives with its inspiring message of hope and confidence in God. Thanks, Bill Gaither!

Because He lives, we can face tomorrow – no matter what comes – miracle or loss – He holds the future, and our hope is in Him.

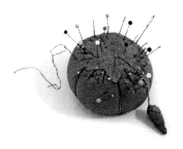

~ 26 ~
Anvil
Submitted by Karrie Vandewater of Stuttgart, Germany

Our family never went to church, and as I child, I received no formal training in the ways of the Lord. I remember my grandmother taking me to a church from time to time. I heard things about God throughout my growing up years, but it was vague and didn't impact my life. I knew little of God's character or the truths of His Word.

Looking back, I believe I tried to find God based on what I knew of Him, and I tended to look for Him in the way I perceived He should be. Unfortunately, in spiritual matters, natural perception is not always correct. The reality is, God never changes, and He will come to us as He is. It is we who many times miss seeing Him because of our own ideas of who we think He should be.

John chapter seven records an account of Jesus' Jewish contemporaries' attempt to figure out who He was. It was true back then, and it is true today: we look for Him through eyes that cannot see or understand. That is where I found myself about fourteen years ago.

My husband and I were both 32 years old. Our sons were six and four at the time. We did not recognize it then, but now when we look back, we realize God had things planned for us we knew nothing about.

We were like everybody else we knew in those days – a young couple looking for happiness through the accomplishments in our lives. But deep down inside, nothing provided the peace we searched for. My husband had a good job, allowing me to leave my career to stay home with the children. We were both involved in physical fitness and traveling. Our weekends were all about having fun. But like many young couples, we just weren't happy. We each had issues from our pasts and had brought those issues into our marriage. We each looked to the other person to be something we were not.

I wanted my husband to meet my every need, and he wanted the same from me, but neither of us wanted to be that person for each other, nor could we be. As you can imagine, over time things got pretty rough between us. Our marriage was in trouble, and it seemed we fought over the same issues every day.

The tables began to turn when my husband Greg got sick. On work days, when the weather was nice, Greg liked to sit in his car and eat his lunch at a nearby park. One particular day he had an unusually bad headache. He used to get many headaches, but this one was different. He must have passed out in the car while eating his lunch, because when he came to, it was an hour and a half later.

He originally thought he just fell asleep, but when he reached for his pop, and it slipped from his hand, he realized he could not hold the cup. It was at this point he thought perhaps he experienced something worse than a headache, and he drove himself to the doctor's office. The doctor examined him and found one half of his body to be weaker than the other which indicated the possibility of a stroke. He sent Greg for an MRI.

In addition to new health concerns, things suddenly changed at Greg's work. He was taken completely by surprise when he learned his department was being eliminated. Rather than being laid off, management offered him an interview with a man in another department. If the man didn't hire him, Greg would no longer have a job.

Greg watched his colleagues as, one by one, they interviewed for new positions. Each one left their interview with the prospect of a new job. Greg went into his interview, but was not offered a job. The manager told Greg he couldn't use him. In a nice way, I guess as nice as you can tell someone, Greg was fired.

Well, for me, this was about all I could take at one time. I knew we faced many obstacles, and I knew that neither of us could solve them on our own. The only thing I could think to do was to pray. These problems were too big for us, but if God was real, certainly He could do something.

God, I prayed, *If you are real, and if you will fix my life, I will serve you. Amen.* It was amazing what happened in a short time after that prayer. A minister came to our door and invited us to his church. I was at the playground with the kids and another minister invited us to his church. My neighbor invited me to her church, and a woman my husband worked with invited us to hers. Out of the blue, all of a sudden we received so many invitations. I knew somehow it was God answering my prayer. Now there was a new problem: which church do we go to?

Aren't all churches basically the same? I wondered. I knew there was one type I had seen before, though I'm not sure where. As I considered the different churches, in my mind I told God, *I will go wherever you want me to go – except that one.* In my lack of understanding God, I used my past to predetermine where I would trust God to lead me.

Greg came home from work that day. He looked very strange, and I knew something was up.

"What's going on?" I asked.

"God spoke to me," he answered. "It wasn't an audible voice, but like an imprint in my mind. He told me to get you and the kids and take you to church."

I was amazed. Greg didn't know about my prayer a few days earlier, but I knew this was God answering me. He even told Greg which church we were supposed visit.

This was a Tuesday night, and the church Greg wanted to visit had a Wednesday service. He had already determined he was going to go whether I did or not, and before he left his job, he had informed his astonished coworker he would be at church the next day.

We walked into church that Wednesday night, and I remember it well. From that point on, miraculous changes occurred.

First and foremost, our marriage was instantly healed. It was so strange. It was like we were in high school all over again. We had those giddy feelings for each other – all the anger and bitterness were totally gone.

Next the doctor called with the results of Greg's MRI. He said there was no stroke and the weakness had disappeared. The doctor had no idea what had happened, but gave Greg a clean bill of health.

The man who told Greg he did not have a position for him called him on the phone and said he had changed his mind. He offered Greg a job in his department.

For many years previous, I suffered with depression – constantly plagued by negative thoughts. It affected my sleeping habits, and at times I felt it too difficult to leave the house. The Wednesday after we first stepped into church I woke up and realized the depression was totally gone.

We couldn't believe all the things happening to us. We knew it must be God. I hadn't even been certain God was real. I remember seeing Bibles from time to time and hearing things about God, but never in my wildest dreams did I think He was really real. But He is . . . and He never changes. He gave us the Bible so we can know Him and know the way to salvation.

And, by the way, the church I predetermined I would not go to – that was the church we walked into on that Wednesday night – the night our lives were changed forever by the Lord Jesus Christ.

�֎

We all come to the Lord with our own paradigms, our own experiences, education and preconceived ideas. Even those raised in solid, Bible-teaching churches have this in common – just with different background material.

I titled Karrie's story with the *Anvil* quilt pattern, because I can just see her scenario played out like a Saturday morning cartoon. Road Runner (beep beep) dashes here and rushes there, running around, looking for a good time, pecking his bird seed . . . all the while Wile Ethelbert Coyote is devising another scheme to catch him. He lures the bird with some seed, then drops an Acme anvil off the top of a cliff to squash him – but the anvil somehow always rebounds and hits the coyote instead. The running gag, the story that kept the cartoon going, was Wile E. Coyote's continual defeat by his own gadgets . . . time after time they *almost* worked.

Life was hitting Karrie and Greg pretty hard when they finally turned to the Lord. I love Karrie's transparency as she shared about her struggle with prejudice towards the very church the Lord wanted to use to bring healing and restoration in her life. Like the anvil gag, Karrie's desire to use her own "gadgets" – her own understanding and concepts, could have kept her from many wonderful blessings. I'm so glad that didn't happen. Karrie and Greg now work with AIDS orphans in Africa with the Reclaim Kids program, touching many lives for the Lord.

An anvil dropped on an unsuspecting bird could cause a great deal of damage. An anvil put to use by a skilled blacksmith is a tool for shaping and forging new, useful things. I pray that all believers lay aside the "anvils" of our own perceptions and open ourselves for all God would like to do in us and through us.

Now, just for fun . . .

If you're on a highway and Road Runner goes beep beep.
Just step aside or you might end up in a heap.
Road Runner, Road Runner runs on the road all day.
Even the coyote can't make him change his ways.

Road Runner, that coyote's after you.
Road Runner, if he catches you you're through.
Road Runner, that coyote's after you.
Road Runner, if he catches you you're through.

That coyote is really a crazy clown,
When will he learn that he never can mow him down?
Poor little Road Runner never bothers anyone,
Just runnin' down the road's his idea of having fun.

Road Runner, that coyote's after you.
Road Runner, if he catches you you're through.
Road Runner, that coyote's after you.
Road Runner, if he catches you you're through.

~ 27 ~
Follow the Leader
Submitted by Julianne Jones of Wanganui, New Zealand

"How would you feel about moving back home?"

My heart hammered in my chest as I glanced at my husband holding our firstborn. We continued walking in silence around the headland where we were enjoying the scenic beauty of the coastal area along the bay. This was our first family holiday since our son's birth four months earlier. Waves crashed along the waterline of the peninsula, and a cool wind blew off the bay, but the chills from the blowing breezes seemed small in comparison to the icy fear working its way through my body.

Is he serious? This is home. I was born and raised in Australia. This is where my ancestors settled generations ago to build new lives for themselves. Why move?

"We could just go for a few years maybe," he spoke into the silence.

A few years? My family is here – our son's grandparents – and great-grandparents. How could I leave?

He dropped the question, and I struggled to put it out of my mind. Surely he hadn't meant anything by it. Probably just one of those idle thoughts we all have from time to time.

But over the years the question resurfaced . . . again and again. Each time I experienced less fear until eventually the fear abated altogether. It was just talk. He was feeling homesick. He'd get over it. There was absolutely no reason to get concerned or upset.

I distracted him. I cheered him up so he would forget about going home. I reminded him that we should be content with what we had. We had another son.

The years passed. Another son joined our family. And another. And yet another. Life was good. We were outgrowing our home and dreaming about finding a larger place. We looked at small acreages, but nothing seemed right.

The question rarely surfaced anymore. We were busy: family, church, work, and school. There was no time to waste thinking about *what ifs*? Then one day during my Bible reading a passage seemed to jump off the page at me. It was as if God was speaking His words right into my heart:

At that time I will gather you; at that time I will bring you home. I will give you honor and praise among all the peoples of the earth when I restore your fortunes before your very eyes. (Zephaniah 3:20 NIV)

I argued with God. *I am home. I don't need to move.* But the feeling God was speaking to me persisted.

I was afraid to share with my husband, but I did nevertheless. Although we had rarely spoken of it, his desire to return home had never lessened. We agreed to seek God's will, and I dared to ask, "Are you prepared to pray that if this is not from God, He would take the desire away?"

"Yes," he answered, "but are you prepared to pray that if it is from God He would strengthen the desire – in both of us?"

If my husband was willing to give up his heart's desire, surely I should be willing to have my desires changed. But it wasn't easy.

Time marched on. Circumstances changed. My husband left his job. He was offered another one. He tried to refuse it – several times – but through the management's persistence, he eventually agreed. "Just until Christmas," he told me when I expressed concern.

I started to entertain the thought that God might just require us to move. Always wanting to be prepared, I searched for information about New Zealand. My findings were not encouraging.

Lord, I prayed, *How can we give up everything we have here? Everything we've worked so hard for? If we sell and move now, we'll never be able to afford a home of our own. Things are so expensive over there. And, anyway, we're just starting to get involved in our church here. We're helping out with youth group and I'm playing the piano again. Surely you aren't asking us to give all that up? What if we never get asked to do anything in another church again? We can't move.*

Again the Lord spoke to me through Scripture:

"For I know the plans I have for you . . . plans to prosper you and not to harm you, plans to give you hope and a future. Then you will call upon me and come and pray to me, and I will listen to you . . ." (Jeremiah 29: 11-12 NIV)

I gave up. I stopped fighting. Who was I to question God's plans? Yet underneath the veneer of acceptance, I still wondered if I would be happy with God's plans. Somehow I lost sight of the last part of God's promise to me. Yes, I believed that He knew the plans He had for my life, but I failed to see how there could be hope and a future in those plans. For my husband perhaps, but me? I didn't think so. I even went so far as to see myself as a modern day martyr.

But things were about to change. One Sunday afternoon after my husband and I debated whether God was really telling us to move, I asked, "Have you ever thought of moving back in with your parents and finding employment in the town where they live?"

"No," he answered.

Memories of his boyhood town had always drawn him. We had always assumed that if we returned it would be to that particular town. We never considered living anywhere else.

"Perhaps we should," I said. "We could stay with your family until we find someplace else."

Suddenly it was as if blindfolds had been removed. The question as to whether he should go alone and send for the rest of us later was no longer an issue. It all seemed so obvious now.

The next day the phone rang. There was a job in his field in the town where his parents lived. Were we interested?

"Do you think I could pray that I get the job without an interview?" my husband asked, tongue in cheek. "This close to Christmas, we can hardly afford for me to fly over."

I laughed. "I think we just have to accept that we're going to have to spend the money if you want the job."

He applied for the job and was indeed interviewed over the phone. The job was his. There was no reason for him to fly over.

Suddenly it was happening. And there were so many things to do. Four weeks were all we had. Four weeks to get the house in order and pack up the paraphernalia of twelve years and seven people. Four weeks to say good-bye to friends and family and church. Four weeks to arrange flights and passports and put the house on the market. And somewhere in the midst of those four weeks, find time to celebrate Christmas and attend end-of-the-year school concerts.

The travel agent laughed when I tried to book the tickets. "It's the summer holidays here. Everyone's going overseas. You should have booked months in advance. There's no way you'll get seven seats on the same flight."

She rang back subdued. "You're all booked. You got the last seven seats on the connecting flight. There are only twenty seats on that flight and there were seven left!"

God is good. It's been over ten years since we left Australia. People warned us about homesickness. They predicted we'd be back within a few years. They were wrong. God showed us quite clearly this is where He wants us to be, and until He says otherwise, this is where we're staying.

The day I booked our flight my husband told me he prayed I would be blessed by the move. At the time I was skeptical, but as I look around I realize that God has blessed me far more abundantly than I ever imagined possible.

I prayed for a home large enough for all seven members of our family – including bathroom facilities. God provided more than we ever asked for.

We have been blessed with a wonderful church family, and the ministry roles I was so afraid to give up have been restored many times over. God continues to direct our steps, and I'm doing things now I never thought I would have the courage to do.

I've watched my family grow and mature, and as I've seen the opportunities they have here, I can only say "Thank you, God."

The phrase "follow the leader" first reminds me of a children's game – a line of laughing kids following behind their chosen leader mimicing his actions until one by one, each child messes up and is removed from the game. The one who followed best becomes the new leader. Now, there's a spiritual lesson in that.

"Follow the leader" also brings to mind the concept of spiritual covering. From kids, to wives, to husbands, to pastors – including governing authorities in the natural and spiritual, we protect ourselves when we respect those who watch over our lives.

Julianne's story is not one of a rebellious wife, but a woman reluctant to leave her home – understandable, for sure. However, when she was unwilling to consider that her plans for her future may differ from her husband's or God's, she lived in fear. When she finally surrendered, opening her heart to the possibility, even though uncertainty remained, the fear subsided. In my mind, that is where the battle was won. And as the story played out, what she feared turned out to be a source of blessing for herself and her family.

The quilt pattern, *Follow the Leader* is a playful design one quilter chose to combine with the *Cross and Crown* pattern. The alternating blocks made a striking visual effect. The patterns interact and create more depth and interest than the single patterns. Likewise, when believers connect follow-the-leader attitudes with the Lord (His sovereignty and His cross), something beautiful happens.

*Love and memories we impart
to quilt the fabric of the heart.*

~ 28 ~
Pinwheel
Submitted by Sharon K. Wilson of Clarkston, Michigan

"I think we made it just in time," the expectant mother said upon entering St. Elizabeth's hospital early in the morning. Her water had broken at 3:00 a.m., and contractions were coming steadily five minutes apart. She smiled thinking she would surely hold her firstborn in her arms soon.

After completing the admission process, she dressed in a stiff hospital gown and climbed into the uncomfortable bed. A nurse in full habit made the initial examination, after which she commented calmly, "Something is wrong; there is an obstruction here. Just a moment, please, and I will call the doctor." The young mother was not the least bit alarmed; she completely trusted the hospital staff.

In just a few minutes she was transferred to a gurney and whisked down the corridor to the x-ray room. Her husband was allowed to see the pictures and, much to his surprise, in place of a head near the birth canal, he saw two tiny, dangling feet.

The couple returned to the labor room, but nothing much was happening. The baby had not dropped, its head still high under the mother's breast bone. Contractions fell off to spasmodic intervals and dilation slowed considerably.

Many hours passed. When the contractions did come, the mother could not concentrate on correct breathing as she had been instructed. The labor pains were intense and difficult to bear. With each contraction, she called on the Lord to help her. The attending nun stood quietly with bowed head beside the young mother as she prayed to her God.

Eventually, after several hours of intense labor, she began to dilate. The doctors pushed repeatedly on her abdomen in their attempts to get the baby in position. Although still not dilated to the required ten centimeters, they decided it was time for the delivery.

The young woman was comforted by a glimpse of her mother and father as a mask was placed over her face. "Breathe deep," she heard someone say, and she immediately fell into a deep sleep. With the use of forceps, baby Susan DeeAnn made her arrival in the world buttocks first on May 6, 1966. She weighed 6 pounds 10 ounces, her head was misshapen by the force and trauma of the birth, but mother and daughter were alive and well.

Before being discharged from the hospital, the doctor informed the young mother that her uterus was very much enlarged. "If you have any heavy bleeding, come immediately to the hospital," he warned.

Little Susan's grandmother stayed in the family's small rented home to help her daughter as she recovered from the traumatic delivery. She did the laundry, cleaned, folded diapers, fixed meals, washed dishes, prepared formula and everything else except feeding and diapering the newborn. That was reserved for the young mother. The baby slept a great deal of the time, so the mother was able to rest and regain her strength.

Nine days after the birth, the mother learned her aunt and uncle were planning a visit to see the new baby. The household was excited and proud to show off their little "angel person," as Grandmother called her. Since she felt so well, the young mother insisted that her mom and husband attend Sunday church service. She said she would throw a roast in the oven, take care of the sleeping baby and everything would be fine.

After fixing the roast and peeling carrots, onions and potatoes, the young mother decided to make a salad. But she didn't stop there. She also prepared baby bottles, made a dessert, set the table and made gravy. She bathed, dressed, fed, burped, and diapered the baby. All was ready.

After the arrival of the guests and the appropriate exclamations of approval and congratulations, everyone sat down to dinner. Prayer was offered in thankfulness for the food and God's goodness. As the prayer ended, the young mother excused herself from the table. She indicated to her mother she thought she might have a problem, and when she stood up, the first gush of blood was so powerful she didn't know if she could make it to the restroom. She began hemorrhaging and the mother carefully put her daughter to bed. The guests left hurriedly.

The surge of blood did not stop. The young father prepared to take his wife to the hospital as the doctor instructed. "Oh, I don't think that's necessary. I'll be just fine if I lie real still and don't move," she said. She was in no hurry to go back to the hospital and she exclaimed, "I'll be fine if I get some rest. I must have been standing too long."

The hemorrhaging continued without abatement and towel after towel was carried to the tub to be rinsed out as a fresh towel took its place on the bed. The young woman became very cold and requested more blankets. Her color waned to a chalky pallor as her life's blood seeped from her body. She heard her husband ask again to take her to the hospital, but it was a 30-40 minute ride, and she thought she'd be fine any minute. The young husband respected her wishes, her mother did not interfere, and she did not go to the hospital.

Although she could hear her husband and mother praying softly, she was surprised when she saw her husband reach for his Bible, get down on his knees and cry loudly for God to undertake on her behalf. Their little house had never heard the likes of that prayer before.

The hemorrhaging continued, and the phone rang. It was the young mother's twin sister calling from out-of-state. "What's wrong with my sister? I know something is wrong," she said. She was given the details of the increasingly severe problem, then hung up to join the family in intercession.

The young mother was light-headed, cold and her fingers and toes were numb. She did not say a word but lay very still Soon the cold progressed to her hands and feet. Her concern grew when she felt the blood draining from her extremities.

She softly said to her husband, "I think we should call for someone to anoint and pray for me." Quickly a call was made to a minister who lived down the street.

It seemed only a moment later the minister entered the bedroom. Without any fanfare, he anointed the head of the young mother and prayed a simple prayer that ended with "...in Jesus' Name. Amen."

Immediately, the hemorrhaging stopped. The minister turned to leave, and the young mother smiled, but did not say a word. She waited and lay very still to make sure the bleeding did not start again. She waited until she was certain and finally she smiled again and said, "It stopped." Then she said, "I think we should thank the Lord." And praise the Lord they did.

I wish I could say I was full of faith and knew without a doubt God would deliver me that day. I did not feel any great spiritual strength; nor did I make any grandiose proclamations of faith and healing. I was young and naïve, and I did not know the danger I was in, but through it all I felt protected. I knew I would be okay. Maybe that's what faith is all about.

�֍

Sharon's story certainly had me on pins and needles – and reminded me of the *Pinwheel* quilt block. In a natural pinwheel, the wind activates the propeller-like paddles, causing them to spin about a central point or pin. A simple toy, many of us remember watching in delight as pinwheels mesmerized us with their spiraling wind dances.

Sharon's simple, childlike faith, the "pin" if you will, held the flying "paddles" secure as they spun about her sickbed. While I read her story, I kept thinking *Go to the hospital! Call the doctor!* But God worked everything out in the end.

Winds blow in all our lives. And although we may have a small faith, perhaps only the size of a mustard seed, that pin-sized faith is big enough to secures life's "flying paddles." And when the Lord blows His Spirit upon our circumstances, a joyful dance or spin in His presence refreshes the soul like nothing else.

~ 29 ~
Hens and Chicks
Submitted by Florence Koski of Covington, Kentucky

Sprawled out on my bedroom floor, I wept and mourned over the loss and pain of the previous year. Sorrow, depression and loneliness took their toll, and my body shook with sobs.

I'll just give up, I thought, wanting to surrender and end the struggle. *How did I get here? What happened?* The questions continued to plague me.

A girl raised in the church, I followed the Lord's teachings and precepts. I used the gifts and talents He gave me in ministry. I knew the Word and all the songs, once singing and rejoicing in worship before the Lord, but I was now unable to lift my head to the One who could help.

As I lay on the floor, I remembered where everything started – where sin broke through the gate of protection and everything began falling to pieces in the vacuum of disobedience.

"Okay everyone we're going to close out the youth meeting with prayer. Let's join hands," I said, addressing the fifteen young boys and girls assembled in the room. Their excitement and fire pleased me as their youth leader. Young myself, only 22, I remembered what it was like growing up and learning to be responsible and accountable for myself.

I reached out as a child to others, inviting them to Sunday school, and did what was expected of me. Over the years, I assumed new ministry roles as youth leader, Sunday school teacher, drummer, praise singer and, one of my favorites, testimony leader for my church. What a privilege to express gratitude to the Lord for all His great works.

I worked earnestly for the Lord, and I began to reap many blessings. The Lord blessed me with a God-fearing husband with goals and desires like my own. We had a wonderful home and a great church. What more could we ask for? Job might have thought the same thing, unaware of the storm brewing just over the horizon. I stood satisfied on my mountain top – mentality and spirituality.

After the wedding, I relocated to Norfolk, Virginia, where my husband was stationed in the Navy. Leaving my close-knit family and the church I grew up in was extremely difficult, but I prepared to make a new life with my husband. We planned to stay in Norfolk after he completed his term with the Navy, but when I received word that my two sisters had turned from God, I felt an urgency to move back home. My husband and I agreed, and we returned to Kentucky.

When I arrived, it seemed like a spiritual tornado had touched down before me – debris was scattered everywhere, fragments of precious memories lying crushed on the ground. The discovery traumatized my spirit, and a discouragement began to seep into my soul.

My sisters! The girls I grew up with praising God together – what had happened to turn their worlds upside down? What caused them to listen to the voice of the enemy? The very lies they thought would give them freedom, ended up taking them captive, robbing them of their joy and innocence.

I took a deep breath and decided to move on to see what was left. It broke my heart to see the once active youth standing on the sidelines devastated by the falls of their spiritual role models. Petrified, they wondered if they would be next.

With my pastor's permission, I took back the leadership of the youth ministry and decided I would watch over the young people so carefully nothing would happen to them. I wanted them to feel safe and alive again. I fussed over them as if they were mine, a self-appointed mother hen. But my good intentions skewed my vision. Instead of God's youth, they became my youth. My wrong attitude, assuming ownership of what belonged to God, swung open the gate of protection allowing bitterness to enter.

Several months into my efforts to rebuild the youth ministry, something happened. Blinded by my own error, slowly but surely, the enemy began to steal, kill and destroy.

Numerically, the youth group grew, but the newcomers didn't stay long. The hearts of the young people began to turn as spirits of suicide and lust lingered. It seemed the more I tried to fight and bind the spirits through prayer, the stronger they became.

One by one, as the young people began to drive and graduate from school, they turned completely from God. In the quiet, in those hours of darkness, the gate of protection squeaked open once again, and anger crept in my spirit.

Only two girls remained in the youth group. And if that wasn't enough, most of the adults were leaving, too. With all the spiritual losses, even my body took a severe blow.

A cyst grew on my left ovary, and it the ovary had to be removed. I no longer cared what happened to me. I began to shut down. God tried to strengthen me, but I refused to be moved. People from all over the world – complete strangers came to my church's doorstep to encourage us. God sent them directly to us, men who had never heard of our church. One man was visiting from India, and he felt directed by God to share his testimony and circle the church with prayer. Men from Louisiana, Kansas, and Texas – old-time leaders came and prophesied, but the purging continued.

Then it happened. The last youth left. I could barely conduct myself when church began that first night afterwards. Paralyzed and mute, I could not lead testimony service or play the drums. I expected to receive sympathy from my spiritual leaders, but most did not understand. It seemed even my husband stood against me.

With this final blow, the gate of protection fell completely off its hinges. Loneliness and full-blown depression forcefully entered. I could no longer stand. I felt numb and unattached. My joy was gone, and the memories of my previous year of victorious living only rubbed salt in my wounds. Slowly, night after night, I cried myself to the freedom sleep provided from the mental torment. But bitterness and anger daily tightened my chains. I sat idle, cold and dormant.

Worse behavior revealed the sickened condition of my heart. After all my years of faithfully following church teaching and spiritual leadership, I questioned and resisted what I'd been taught. Because of my defiance, even my pastor contemplated leaving the church. The spirit of rebellion lingered, and I became its agent.

Although I allowed my mental anguish to lead me down a bitter path, I still attended church. One night after a stirring service, I realized I couldn't continue living this way. I knew it was impossible to try to go any further on my own. I thought I could build my own wall of protection, but I ended up in a heap on the floor of my bedroom, crying in desolation. Then I heard the voice of God.

When the enemy comes in like a flood. I will lift up a standard against him.

Just to hear His voice again comforted my spirit, and hope surged in my heart. God had not rejected me, though I turned my back on Him. He was there, and He compassionately re-hinged my fallen gate. It was on the floor of my bedroom in a puddle of tears that I chose to live again in the security and peace that comes from living in right relationship with God – regardless of my circumstances or the choices of others. Three years later, I am now able to share my experience and encourage others to keep their perspectives straight. A mere mortal cannot assume ownership of what belongs to God. He is in control, the One True and Living God.

�֍

After reading Florence's story, I had to get some follow-up, and I'm happy to share that God is working in her church. New people are coming in, and the congregation is growing, abiding in God's truth, and holding on to the promises of God knowing He will do what He said He will do.

Florence's story, titled with the quilt pattern *Hens and Chicks*, reminds us that we are only able to control our own choices. No matter how heartbreaking – no matter how much we care about others, or how much we attempt to protect them, the truth remains: God gave men and women free wills to make their own decisions in life.

Holding on to our own convictions becomes more challenging when we watch others around us fall. From everything to dieting to serving God, in the end, we are accountable only for our own decisions. From brownie binging to spiritual backsliding – no matter who else falls off the bandwagon, we stand in our own integrity and choices before the Lord.

However, the choices we make do affect those around us. So I encourage you today to hold on to the Truth and be an example for others. May our conduct inspire those around us to pursue excellence, dream big and be all we can be for the Lord and each other . . . especially our own little chicks.

❋

Our lives are like quilts –
bits and pieces,
joy and sorrow,
stitched with love.

~ 30 ~
Dancing Bear
Submitted by Steve Lockman of Lancaster, Minnesota

My father joined the Marines shortly after I was born. After basic training at the U.S. Marine Corps Base in Camp Pendleton, California, he came home long enough to conceive my sister, who was born 1 year and 14 days after me.

The 1st Marine Division, including my father, shipped out to Okinawa in April 1945 where they faced the last battle against the Japanese in the Pacific. Neither my sister nor I remember dad at all. Mother never saw him again.

Before he left the country, my father named his mother beneficiary of his life insurance policy. When he was killed, she received the proceeds which she used to buy a new stove and refrigerator. Mother, apparently overwhelmed with grief, left my sister and me with our father's parents. We learned years later she moved to Kansas City where she lived with a man and had another son.

Grandfather died when my sister and I were 9 and 10 respectively. With only a third grade education, Grandma secured a job washing dishes in a downtown St. Paul restaurant earning $25 a week. That's when the welfare department stepped in and placed my sister and me in different foster homes. Eight years passed before we saw each other again.

I had several placements in the foster care system, one in which I found myself living in the country in a dirt floor chicken coop. For almost a year I survived on peanut butter sandwiches and pickles. I never had a hot meal in all that time. I appeared anorexic, but was in reality malnourished.

In one of my previous placements I had been repeatedly beaten and sexually molested. It seemed I had been abandoned – by everyone except my Lord and Savior Jesus Christ. Thankfully, Grandmother introduced my sister and me to Him before we were taken from her home, because knowing Him gave me the strength and hope to survive.

After the chicken coop experience, I have to say the homes that followed were an improvement, but I never really became part of a family. It seemed most families took foster kids in as a business venture. At least that was my experience.

One man who took me in was a policeman – apparently not a very popular one. Because I was living with him, I started getting beat up in the school bathrooms, after school, and at football games, etc., simply because he was a cop. It was so bad I dropped out of school, and at 17 I took a GED test and received my high school equivalency certificate.

Finally on my own, I forged a new life for myself in the Minneapolis area. I met and married my wife Betty and we had two beautiful daughters. In my early 20s I began to exhibit symptoms of a neuromuscular disorder. Over time, Limb-Girdle Muscular Dystrophy confined me to a wheelchair with disabling muscle and joint pain.

Through it all, I still had faith that God was with me. I went to see a "faith healer" – an elderly lady who lived in a farmhouse with her husband. She was somewhat grotesque in appearance. Years before she had cut cancerous growths from her face with a razor blade. Her nose was gone, most of her lips and ears, and other parts of her face were disfigured. She had been diagnosed and sent home to die. No treatments were available at the time. She told me she had prayed to God for a cure and had been told to save herself, so she cut the cancer out and lived.

The old woman laid her hands on me and began to pray "in the Name of Jesus." When she finished, she looked at me and smiled. I stared at her face in amazement – it was beautiful, without blemishes.

After the prayer, she told me that my miracle would be of the spirit, and that though my body would not be restored while on this earth, my strength and salvation would be found through the love of our merciful Father in Heaven. She said that if I sought His truth and guidance, I would find joy and happiness throughout my life, despite my physical condition.

I wish I could say I unfailingly followed her advice. At times I allowed my circumstances to overwhelm the truth of the promises she gave me. In these times I suffered greatly. But each time the bottomless pit of despair loomed before me, beckoning me to fall in and give up, I recalled her words, "You will find your strength and salvation through the love of our Father in Heaven."

On one occasion, as I prayed for forgiveness and strength, I felt myself lifted out of the darkness. A tangible presence of the Lord effortlessly pick up my adult, disabled body and carried me towards a Light that filled my whole being with warmth, security, hope and joy. I had been given another miracle.

I've seen some bad days, and still deal with the affects of physical disability, but I believe in miracles and see them all around me. A miracle is not always seeing someone walk away from a wheelchair, or the elimination of arthritic pain, or the sightless being able to see. The greatest and most abundant miracles are those unseen – those experienced in the heart and mind and soul.

Therefore we do not lose heart. Though outwardly we are wasting away, yet inwardly we are being renewed day by day. For our light and momentary troubles are achieving for us an eternal glory that far outweighs them all. So we fix our eyes not on what is seen, but on what is unseen. For what is seen is temporary, but what is unseen is eternal. (2 Corinthians 4:16-18 NIV)

I've walked . . . and rolled . . . through some hellish days, but by the power of God's forgiveness and mercy, He continues to restore my mind and spirit. And one day His love will bring me home.

�֍

I met Steve through a book I was reading on starting your own business at home. Green and excited, I wrote a "spiffy" introductory letter asking his advice as I began my at-home word processing service. I still have his letter from 17 years ago encouraging me to pursue my dreams and offering me his help. He made me feel special and hopeful as I embarked on my entrepreneurial journey.

Communicating through the mail and over the phone, quite some time passed before I learned the successful, competent man with the booming baritone voice had anything but sunshine and rainbows in his life. When I did learn of his physical challenges, I admired him all the more and coaxed bits of information from him about his experiences from the chicken coop to appearing on the Jerry Lewis telethon.

Steve is one of my heroes – a large, gentle man bearing much on his broad shoulders. The quilt pattern *Dancing Bear* may seem an odd selection for Steve's story, but I have to tell you, that I am looking at Steve through "miracle eyes."

Dancing bears are taken from their mothers when they are young. Their handlers pierce their mouths enabling the men to run chains through the openings and train the animals to dance as they attempt to avoid the pain of the chains tugging on their raw wounds. Many die of dehydration or starvation, but those that survive learn to dance.

Steve learned to dance, and one day, he's going to be separated from disability's chains. His huge heart will lift from his bear-sized frame and receive a new, perfect body . . . and I believe he will dance some more in the arms of the Lord. Until then, I thank God for bringing Steve into my life and for the example he's been to me.

Whatever chains tug at the wounds life inflicts upon us, we can learn to dance, too, and remember, like Steve, that this world is only a temporary dwelling place. We have a bright future in Christ.

~ 31 ~
Treasure Chest
Submitted by Jan Ross of Willard, Ohio

Last year my husband lost his job. After a 30-year history of consistent employment with the same company, we suddenly found ourselves faced with downsizing and taking a hard look at the future.

At the time, Ron's mom was very ill. She had been living with one of my brothers-in-law but wanted very much to spend her last days in her own home – the house her husband built for her in 1952. It seemed the right thing to do given our situation, so my husband and I sold our house to our youngest daughter and relocated 100 miles away to the old family home.

The original homestead included two houses – the one Ron grew up in and his grandmother's house across the field. Living in the old house, I discovered treasures I never would have known if Ron hadn't lost his job.

One day I cleaned out a closet and found a bundle of old handmade quilts. I carefully washed and hung them out on the line to dry in the sun. One was particularly lovely, and as I pinned it on the line I knew I wanted to learn more about this Flower Garden quilt. Later that afternoon, I stacked the clean, fresh quilts back in the spare bedroom, not grasping the treasure I was about to discover.

"Mom, are you awake?"

From her reclining position in a plush easy chair, my mother-in-law responded with a peaceful smile, her eyes still closed and her hands folded quietly on her lap.

"Yes, honey. What time is it?"

"It's 2:30," I answered. "I was wondering if you were up to talking a bit. I cleaned out a closet and found more quilts and afghans. I don't know how you found time for all that needlework in the middle of raising a family, working full time, keeping up with Grandma, and staying involved in church."

Mom just smiled. I noticed her fingers moving on her lap . . . unconsciously replaying the stitching or hooking that filled so much of her time in earlier years.

"Can you help me to the bedroom?" she asked. "I'd like to look at some of the quilts again."

I walked over, pushed the button on her lift chair and assisted her to her feet. Grabbing her oxygen tank with one hand, I held out my free arm. She took it, steadied herself, and slowly we made our way to the spare bedroom where I eased her into a comfortable chair. Tucking a freshly laundered afghan around her legs, I sat on the bed and waited for her to begin.

"Do you remember the big room upstairs in Grandma's house – right at the head of the stairway?"

"Oh yes! How could I forget?" I answered. "It's a huge room with a feather bed, chest of drawers, and an old sewing machine. And, several handmade chairs – I remember them especially. Grandpa's handiwork, I suppose."

I noticed a sparkle in Mom's eyes I hadn't seen in quite a while. She continued, "Before you were born, honey, that room was the center of activity every winter. It was the time of year we looked forward to most. The crops were in, canning completed, children in school, husbands busy discussing the latest news and maintaining their farm implements . . . and us women got together to make quilts."

"Is it true there's a story to go with each quilt?" I asked.

"Oh, honey! My memory is not so good. But, take out that quilt – see the one in the middle with the soft pink and blue flowers on it? There's a story that goes with that quilt. Maybe if you unfold it I can remember."

I reached into the pile and pulled out the beautiful Flower Garden quilt I admired earlier. Unfolding it carefully, I spread it across the bed and ran my fingers over the intricate stitching.

"So tell me, Mom, what's the story behind this quilt?"

She closed her eyes and laid her head back against the chair as if to take a trip back in time, then she began . . .

At the first sign of winter, Grandma cleared out the big room upstairs – except for the chairs, cutting table and quilting frame. As soon as she put up her last quart of tomatoes, she started preparing, looking for scraps of colorful fabrics and assembling her notions. A story went with each scrap of material, and it would be shared with the womenfolk when they gathered themselves for the quilting.

Grandma looked forward to that time of year. The bugs were gone, but there was always a buzz of activity in the house. With her kids all grown and having families of their own, those of us who lived nearby enjoyed getting together when we could.

Grandpa always kept the potbelly stove red hot on those cold days. It was on the first floor, but there was a vent right above it that released warm air into the upstairs room. We never got cold, even on the snowiest days or when the wind rattled the glass in the windows.

Grandma was good at finding the perfect fabrics for quilting. I loved to watch her. But the most fun in working with Grandma was hearing the stories that went with each scrap. As we busied ourselves with stitching, she'd tell us where each piece came from – Grandpa's shirts, pants and undergarments, old dresses and children's clothes that had been patched one too many times to be worn – all found their way into Grandma's quilt squares.

Let's see, looking at that quilt now, seems I remember Grandma telling us about a local family who faced a horrible tragedy – they lost their three little girls in a fire. I wish I could remember more of the details.

Anyway, ladies came from neighboring farms to join in the sewing. Grandma served hot tea and some of her homemade cinnamon bread while we decided what kind of quilts to make that winter. Someone suggested that Flower Garden pattern. It sounded like a good place to start.

Now, honey, I'm not sure if I remember this right or not, but I think those pretty blue and pink and white petals in the flowers on that quilt are actually cut from dresses worn by the little girls who died in that fire I told you about. Seems like that's what I remember, but I can't be sure. I do remember that quilt represents pain and loss and suffering. But, it also stands for healing and joy and restoration. Looking at it now, I still get a sense of the pain and sorrow the family experienced, but that quilt brought some hope into their lives. Those flowers stitched with love and prayers of caring friends reminded the dear souls of the beauty of life and the promise of the resurrection to come through Jesus.

Now that I think on it, I recall that particular quilt was given to Grandma after the lady down the road passed on. You know, I look at the quilts and still see the faces, hear the voices, and feel the love we shared in Grandma's upstairs room. That's what makes each quilt so special. Promise me you'll take care of them and pass them down to your children and grandchildren.

Tired from all the talking, Mom picked up a tissue and wiped the tears from her eyes. I wished I could climb into her memories and see what she had seen, experience the mixture of joy and sadness and every day life shared by the women in Grandma's upstairs room on those cold wintry days.

Mom's mind had been going for some time, her lucidity rare, but she was able to share much in the next few days. As I unfolded the quilts, she told their stories: births, weddings, tragedy that gave way to victory, childhood dreams fulfilled, and unbelievable loss made bearable through love.

Mom went on to be with the Lord not many days after our journey through the quilts, but the memory of Grandma's attic and the chattering ladies busily quilting and sharing their lives continues now in me and in the quilts they left behind. What a treasure we've been given . . . a closet full of handmade quilts preserving a legacy of love and prayer along with the precious memories of quilting in Grandma's upstairs room.

When my husband lost his job, we thought it was a tragedy, but it turned out to be one of the best things that ever happened to us. He went nearly an entire year without employment, but God sustained us, and the riches we found learning the family history, the deep Christian heritage left us and all the treasures we keep finding have made the whole experience so very worthwhile.

✖

Jan's story speaks clearly of the true blessings and treasures of life. When her husband lost his job, their plans changed in a moment – unexpectedly. I'm sure in some way, we have all faced similar situations. Life hijacks our agendas, and we learn we aren't as "in control" as we like to think.

In my research for this book, I have seen hundreds of quilt photos. Some of my favorites are draped across heirloom rockers and chests, or stacked in antique bureaus. As I enjoyed these photos I thought of Jan's story and the blessings, the treasures each handmade quilt carries from one generation to the next. Even those that lost their identities still carry a mysterious message. Who made them? Where did the fabric come from? What went on in the heart and mind of the one who held the work so many hours?

For some reason, I just can't picture mean, nasty old ladies making quilts – flawed people, yes, as we all are – but there is something endearing about the process. Perhaps, because it requires so much from the quilter a selfish person would not have to give. "A good man out of the good treasure of the heart bringeth forth good things." (Matthew 12:35)

❁

As a knot appears unexpectedly in a thread,
so disappointment blocks the smoothness of life.
If a few deft strokes can untangle the skein,
life continues evenly.
But if it cannot be corrected,
then it must be quietly woven into the design.
Thus the finished piece can still be beautiful -
although not exactly as planned.
~ Author Unknown

~ 32 ~
Job's Tears
Submitted by Brad Erlandson of Clarkston, Michigan

I was nineteen and immersed in the 70s drug culture when I experienced a dramatic conversion to Christ. Some would say I was not deeply involved in the drug scene, but I knew if I continued on the path I was on I would soon be in prison or dead.

After my conversion I plunged headlong into the Christian world. I knew nothing of theology or doctrine; all I knew is I had an experience that changed my life. Hungry for Truth, I went to Bible college and earned a Masters in Religion. I studied diligently, anxiously absorbing the Word as much and as fast as I could.

Over time, I began to observe disagreements among Christians on various issues. It was unsettling, because I really wanted to know The Truth. If we all serve the same God, why don't we have the same convictions and doctrines?

One issue that concerned me was the plight of human suffering. A skeptic asked me the question, "If God is all loving and all powerful, why doesn't He eliminate human suffering?" Continuing with this line of reasoning, he concluded that God is neither all powerful or all loving – a theory confirmed in his mind by all the suffering in the world. I didn't know how to respond.

As time and experience brought the question, so they provided my answer. I learned through a life-changing event that the question itself was not correct. Instead of questioning God's power and love, we should ask, "What is the purpose of life?" When we answer this question, then we can understand the suffering issue more clearly.

At 6:30 p.m., on April 26, 2002, I was struck head-on by a drunk driver on my way home from work. I sustained multiple rib and vertebra fractures and a closed-head injury that crossed my mental wires for a time. My spleen ruptured and had to be removed. But the worst was yet to be revealed – a spinal cord injury paralyzed me from the waist down.

Since that time I have been doing my best to get back as much feeling and movement as I can. Many people continue to pray for my healing. I go to an aggressive rehab program four days a week, but as of the time of this writing I still cannot walk without the assistance of braces. I can do many things I was told by professionals I would never do again, but I cannot walk . . . yet.

This brings me to the point I want to emphasize. The Bible tells us about a man named Job. By God's pronouncement Job was a righteous man. ". . .There is none like him on earth, a blameless and upright man . . ." (Job 1:8) This is God talking. He bragged on Job then allowed him to go through severe trials.

Job lost his children, his possessions and then his health. Once a powerful and strong man, he fell into seclusion and weakness. But that is not the end of the story. Although Job suffered terribly for a season, God restored his losses many times over. Beyond the blessings of family, wealth and health, Job learned to see God in a new way. He said, ". . . I know that You can do everything, and that no purpose of Yours can be withheld from You . . . I have heard of You by the hearing of the ear, *but now my eye sees You . . .*" (Job 42:2, 5 NKJV)

The Apostle Paul was a man called by God to establish the early church. He suffered many things at the hands of those who did not believe, yet he writes, "And we know that all things work together for good . . . for whom He foreknew, He also predestined to be conformed to the image of His Son . . . what shall we then say to these things, if God be for us who can be against us? (Romans 8:28,29,31 NKJV) Three things are present here: God is for us not against us, suffering is a part of the walk of faith, and it is all designed to make us more like Jesus.

I have been part of "faith" churches for the last three decades, but I never bought the idea that if you're a "real Christian" you will never suffer – you'll be infinitely supplied with health and wealth. When all the tragedies hit Job, his response was, "Naked I came from my mother's womb, and naked I shall return there. The Lord gave and the Lord has taken away; blessed be the name of the Lord." (Job 1:21 NKJV)

What I have learned through my situation is that my faith has to be in the God of the Bible – not a made up Disney god some teach. I don't understand, but I am not called to – or to figure it all out. Like Job, I am called to believe the Word – "that no purpose of Yours can be withheld from You."

Many times in my agony – physical and spiritual – I screamed out to God. *Why have you allowed this? Why?*

Like Israel, I was delivered from bondage by the Lord. In the time between Israel's deliverance from Egypt and their habitation in the Promised Land, they lived on manna, which means "what's this?" God brought Israel out of slavery, but when they were fed manna for a long period of time they grumbled and complained. They were willing to return to slavery just to have better things to eat.

I like health and prosperity . . . most do. Given a choice who would not choose health over sickness? Prosperity over poverty? When hard times come into our lives, like the Israelites in the desert, we ask, "What's this?" How does this fit into the "plan" which we subconsciously think is the "good life" of health and prosperity?

Paul said, ". . . for I have learned in whatever state I am, to be content; I know how to be abased and I know how to abound . . ." (Phil 4:11-12 NKJV) Thank God contentment can be learned. "I have learned," Paul said. After all this time, I am still learning. I have not arrived, but I am in the process. Some days I have the feeling that everything will all work out, and other days I wonder what reason I have to go on.

If I believed that as a Christian I should face no adversity, my faith would have been destroyed long ago. By faith, I embrace the God of the Bible and am encouraged by the many men and women in the Bible who endured hard circumstances.

Answer the question of purpose, and the realities of pain and suffering take on different meaning. When the question of purpose is properly answered, it helps us put our situations in proper perspective. Though hardship is never easy, at least with God's help we can believe He is with us – and for us – and in His time He will bring us where He wants us to be.

Job's losses were restored (Job 42:12-15), Jacob got a new name (Genesis 32:13-32), and David after many years of running from King Saul was installed as King (1 and 2 Samuel). Jesus Christ was raised from death itself, and He promises all who believe will live forever with Him and in Him (John 3:16).

We may not see everything we want in this life in terms of restored losses, but Peter encourages with these words, "In this you greatly rejoice, though now for a little while, if need be, you have been grieved by various trials, that the genuineness of your faith being more precious than gold that perishes, though it is tested by fire, may be found to praise, honor, and glory at the revelation of Jesus Christ." (1 Peter 1:6-7 NKJV)

It seems that some of our reward in heaven will be based on how we deal with the hard times that come to us on earth. I still believe God can and will heal me (in this life or the next), and I take comfort in the Scriptures that speak of the benefits of trials and God's hand upon His people as they go through them.

In the trials, we have to make up our minds that we will not become bitter toward God . . . or men . . . or ourselves. Through faith, because of our trials, we can become better. *Bitter or better* – a simplistic cliché – but that really is the choice. And we are not alone in our hard places. God is with us, helping us along the way. That's what I hold on to every day – and it (He) works.

Researching the *Job's Tears* quilt pattern, I discovered two variations. The first features a cross spanning each block with four triangular "tears" in the openings. A square center stitched at the intersection of the cross represents Job in the midst of his fragmented life.

The second pattern has interconnecting "tear drops" resembling four-petaled daisies with circular centers that stretch across open white fields. Zooming in on one of the photos of this pattern, I saw something I missed at first glance. What appeared to be an overly simple design held an unexpected visual treat. Within the abundance of white space, the quiltmaker stitched intricate needlework in arresting designs. Swirls, swoops, flowers, vines, leaves, and fans spun out here and there dancing in abstract across the barren fields between the tears. Likewise, when we look a little deeper at the quilt of our lives, we may discover hidden treasures the Quilter diligently, meticulously, purposely included in what appear to be empty places.

Learning the right questions to ask is an important life lesson. In my own body, I have not faced the challenge that Brad has to deal with, but when I was going through a difficult situation, the Lord clearly instructed me with a message similar to what He revealed to Brad.

Don't ask "why?" . . . *ask "what?"* the Lord impressed on my heart.

"OK," I said. "I get it." With this direction, I was able to refocus, and it totally changed my perspective and attitude from one of self-pity to an opportunity to grow and learn more about God.

I asked:

What am I supposed to learn from this situation?

What am I supposed to do in response to this situation?

What growth can I achieve from this situation?

Brad's story, titled after the quilt pattern *Job's Tears*, is sprinkled throughout with Scripture. The Word is what keeps us in times of darkness. It is our guiding Light. And although walking with the

Lord sometimes seems like the "school of hard knocks," there is purpose in pain.

At times life does hit hard, but God's intentions and responses to our emotions are kind (even discipline is based in love). Scripture says the Lord catches every tear in a bottle. Imagine a big apothecary in heaven – its shelves lined with beautiful glass jars and decanters labeled with our names and filled with our tears. Our compassionate God cares about our suffering.

But more than our comfort, He cares for the condition of our souls – our character – our eternal destinies. Through our trials we learn to SEE God for who He is . . . not who we want Him to be, or hope He might be. At the end of our trials, I pray we share the understanding Brad has come to and Job expressed when he said, "I have heard of You by the hearing of the ear, but now my eye sees You . . ." (Job 42:5)

~ 33 ~
Beggar's Block
Submitted by Karen Elengikal of Sydney, Australia

My eyes snapped open. I had been in a deep sleep, and at first did not realize where I was. *Oh . . . yes, India,* I remembered. Slumber's fog melted in the stifling heat. It was early, around 7:00 a.m., and already the tropical sun bore down making sweat run freely on my skin.

Yeah! I rejoiced when I noticed the fan spinning slowly overhead. *We have electricity today.* Rolling to my side, I pushed up from the bed, plunked swollen feet on the floor and slowly rose to check on my family. They slept peacefully. All was well.

I waddled across the main hall toward the kitchen. *Wonder if we have water.* With a last sleepy yawn, I turned the metal handle, pleased by the trickle issuing from the tap. *Ah . . . water! Thank You for this blessing today, Lord!*

I love early morning. Fresh and uncluttered by life's demands, my spirit drinks in the moments of quiet before the rush of the day begins. *I'll just open this window and let in the morning air,* I thought as I prepared to submerge myself in solitude and enjoy a cup of tea before my husband and sons rose for the day. With some difficulty, I leaned my bulk across the deep kitchen sink to unlatch the windows. My prolific stomach in the way, I lunged forward, pried open the tiny latches that released the steel security bar and flung the windows open.

"Ahhhgggg!" I screamed as I looked outside. A wild man was standing right outside my window – and he was looking at me.

I recognized him. He was the old beggar I'd often seen on the main road to town rummaging through garbage for scraps of

171

food – a worn out figure lugging a soiled duffle bag behind him that contained all his worldly possessions. *He's never been here before . . . at my house! What's he doing here?*

The dirty, unkempt beggar gestured wildly and threw incoherent words at me. *Dear God, is he going to attack me? I can't understand what he's saying.* Panicked, I called for reinforcements.

"Geeooorge!" I bellowed from my station at the kitchen window, unable to flee on feet paralyzed by fear.

Abruptly awakened by my screams, my darling husband George leapt from bed and rushed into the kitchen to save me. Disheveled and still groggy, my knight in rumpled pajamas was ready to annihilate whatever bug or large hairy spider he assumed to be the reason for my cries. He was as shocked as I when he discovered the cause of my alarm – the frenzied beggar man grunting and groaning at me through the kitchen window.

Breathe. Relax. George is here now. I calmed myself as my husband went outside to talk to the pitiful man. Numerous questions coursed through my mind, *What's he doing here? Why is he yelling at me through the window? Doesn't he realize how scary he looks?*

My mental investigations suspended with a crisp directive from George. "He's hungry. Make him some food and tea – fast."

Responding to George's urgency, I quickly heated leftovers from the previous evening's meal and brewed fresh Indian tea – my own need for a "cuppa" suspended for the moment. As I moved about the kitchen readying the food and drink, I heard George sharing the gospel with the poor, wretched man. My heart was moved with compassion, and I began to pray.

They were in front of the compound. I placed the food and tea on a tray and carried it out with a prayer of blessing. Then I retreated, giving the starving man space to eat his meal in privacy.

The child forming in my womb suddenly moved, and I affectionately rubbed my bulging belly, delighting in the miracle of new life. I lifted my eyes to the beggar once more and scanned his face and figure. He was very old and obviously sick. He wore rags and his skin was caked in filth.

The hungry man swiftly devoured every last morsel of food then sipped his tea while George continued talking to him, sharing with him the love of God. The thought that he might leave our house unsaved overwhelmed me, and I became burdened with the weight of it crushing my spirit. Fervent prayer rushed from my heart for his salvation. *Here and now, Lord! He may not have a tomorrow!*

But after he finished the tea, the nameless beggar heaved himself from the ground and left to attend his other beggarly duties. George and I watched him slowly lumber up the street toward the main road, his usual dwelling place.

"That's the first time he ever came here," I said to George, "I'm so glad he came. How did he respond to the Lord?"

"I've been praying specifically for that man for some days," George replied. "He will die soon. The Lord directed him here so he can be saved before he dies. He has heard the gospel and believes in Jesus."

Tears streamed down our faces. Speechless, we were overwhelmed by the depths of God's love and mercy for a shunned beggar – forgotten and ignored by men, but not by his Creator.

My mind swirled with all the events leading up to that morning. George, inspired by God, had prayed for an unknown beggar's salvation. The Holy Spirit compelled the beggar to leave his search for food in the rubbish heaps he usually foraged, and instead he visited our house. Having been prepared through prayer, George was ready to share the gift of salvation with this dying man. I wondered if the poor beggar knew that Almighty God had ordered his steps to my kitchen window, a divine orchestration by a merciful God.

That was the last we saw or heard of that man – one beggar among millions. One life touched, but for an eternity.

❋

Like Karen, I love the morning quiet. I can just imagine this scene: a very pregnant lady, smiling and stretching, greets the new day with the anticipation of a few tranquil minutes alone. She opens her window to a frightful sight – a groaning, incomprehensible, dirty man. Someone who threatens her safety and repulses her natural senses.

But that's not what God saw. He saw a man with multiple needs – food, comfort and the good news of Jesus Christ – and He connected the poor man with people who could supply them. God cares for each of us regardless of our condition, and the cleanest person – smelling good and looking fine – still needs the purifying touch of God.

Karen's story was titled after the *Beggar's Block* quilt which received its name from the activity surrounding the gathering of materials to make it. These quilts incorporate scraps of fabric "begged" from friends, family and neighbors to create a quilt commemorating friendships and close ties.

In our lives we may not come in contact with a man in the condition Karen faced, but needy people surround us. I pray the Lord opens our eyes to see the needs of the people we come in contact with. Alone, you and I cannot supply every need, but, like *Beggar's Block* quilts, we can pool our resources to accomplish much.

~ 34 ~
Cathedral Window
Submitted by Christine Gibson of Rochester Hills, Michigan

"You aren't like other white people."

Huh? The look on my face must have prompted my Chinese neighbor Qui (pronounced *chew*) to elaborate. She continued as her toddler practiced walking between us in front of her home.

"I mean, you talk to Asians. You were eating dinner with Indians and Germans yesterday on your deck. Most whites are polite to us, but they just say hello and aren't really interested in getting to know people different than they are. You are so nice to foreigners."

As these unusual comments settled into my brain, I realized with delight, how much God had changed my attitude about our neighbors over the last five years. I answered my friend with a smile, "You know, that is because we believe God actually chose you to be our neighbor!"

Many of our foreign neighbors are consistently open and friendly to us, and my husband and I try to respond to them the same way. We believe God ordered our steps bringing our family to this community and are convinced He orchestrated international moves to bring specific individuals from the ends of the earth to live near us. Not because we are so special – we sure have our bumps and wrinkles – but because we pray for our neighbors and want them to truly experience Jesus' love through our relationships.

When we cleared our lot and built our home, dense woods and wetlands surrounded our new residence. The few houses around were several lots away. As my husband toiled, spending

175

much of 1997 constructing our house, I prayed daily, asking God to plunk believers and unbelievers ready to hear the Gospel right in our new neighborhood.

At first, it was a selfish prayer. I was tired of being the only Christian stay-at-home mom in a neighborhood where most of the other women my age packed up and left for work every morning, and the kids for daycare. I dreamed of lots of Christians living and helping each other, sharing outdoor time, even having Bible studies in our homes together . . . kind of like the book of Acts, where the line between "church" and "neighborhood" blurred.

In my dreaming, I envisioned other families that looked and acted like mine.

I continued praying and trying to listen to God's directives for my family. Over time, the Lord moved my vision beyond my personal needs and desires for my family. I learned to embrace His plan and realized His faithfulness was greater than I ever imagined.

Construction finished, inspections passed, and van unloaded, the Gibson clan assumed residency of our new home. Not long after, I opened the front door for my first neighborhood ramble. I love to walk and clipped along at a comfortable pace until I reached a dirt road where a man played with his young daughter. I could tell by his home and the amount of bicycles in the front yard that he had a large family. He said hello and before I knew it, I found myself saying, "I've been praying to meet your family! I've been praying for a year that we'd have Christian neighbors!" Our families are still dear friends nine years later. God clearly and specifically answered my prayers. But, He had so much more in store.

The land surrounding our new house was sold to a developer, and within 18 months, 90 four-bedroom homes went up. This wasn't exactly the "little house in the big woods with Christian neighbors" I had dreamed of.

Families from India, Romania, Korea, China, Germany, France, Russia, New Zealand, Israel and other Middle Eastern countries settled within a block of our home – most recruited from outside the U.S. by the auto industry.

We began to smell new foods and spices around dinner time, hear new dialects, see new clothing styles, and observe all sorts of different customs. Our children started playing with children that looked quite different than they did, but children have a way of accepting each other without hesitation, and they quickly formed new friendships. I adjusted to hearing Chinese, German and Romanian words mixed into my own children's conversations.

While I've always enjoyed reading biographies of missionaries, neither my husband nor I felt directed to this calling. And yet, God provided a mission field right in our own back yard. It took time for God to change our thinking, but now we know that we are missionaries as He reaches others through the relationships He brings into our lives. Not all of our neighbors are open to us, and for some of them respecting their desire for privacy is the best way we can love them at this time.

Once our children became playmates with our neighbors I wondered if we could really relate to people so very different from us. Some were absolute atheists, having left countries where religion had been forced on them. Others were deeply rooted in cultures where religion and family were indivisibly integrated and change in religious beliefs would compromise family ties.

Initially, this former home schooler wrestled with the question of allowing my little lambs to play with children who had altars and idols in their homes. The more I prayed for my neighbors, the more my personal prejudices fell away and the less "different" they seemed. The more we interacted, the more I saw them as I saw myself: a sinner desperately dependent on God's grace.

There was a time I would not have been open to eating a meal in my Hindu neighbor's home, especially at a table next to an altar room full of golden idols, photos of ancestry being worshiped and food offerings. But God removed my fear. My family belongs to Him. We are His children, pilgrims in this present world.

One thing my family committed to regarding our neighbors is there were to be no strings attached on our relationships. We aim to be the best neighbors and friends we can, regardless of their response to the Gospel.

After four years of friendship, eating and walking together, lending tools back and forth, helping with projects and just being good neighbors and friends, one dear Hindu family allowed their teen to accept and read a Bible from our teen. Another Chinese Christian neighbor asked us how they could increase their faith in God. An unsaved teen from a broken home attends our family Bible studies faithfully – and feels like another son in our home.

God does allow us to see fruit in others at times, but we love others as a response to His love towards us. Seeing the fruit is a reward, but not our motive.

Our commission is to love others. We leave the eternal results up to God. We are His laborers: He owns the vineyard. What an awesome honor and privilege it is to represent Him to others. May God direct, guide and make good use of all His people, wherever He places them.

Then I saw another angel . . . and he had the eternal gospel to proclaim to . . . every nation, tribe, language and people. Worship Him who made the heavens, the earth, the sea and the springs of water. (Rev. 14:6-7 NIV)

※

I share Chris's story with great joy and appreciation for her sweet spirit and servant's heart. She is a humble person with a burning passion to share the good news of Jesus with others. It was through her witness on the job that my sister was saved, and my sister, in turn, brought me to a church where I met the Lord.

I've never seen Chris's house, but I have an image in my mind of her windows. Though not of intricate design or composed of stained glass, I envision them as cathedral windows – windows her family looks out of and sees a world to reach, and windows the lost look into and find hope.

The *Cathedral Window* quilt pattern utilizes a unique "fabric folding" technique. Traditionally, the window panes are made of a neutral muslin or cheesecloth that set the stage for colorful diamond-shaped inserts. The pattern is most lovely when created as a "charm" quilt – when each "window" opening features a different color and pattern all hand sewn into place.

The *Cathedral Window* quilt pattern, with it's variety of color and pattern uniformly stitched in an intricate design, reminds me of the diversity of race and peoples we will see in Heaven and the personal touch required to bring each "diamond" into the "fold."

The Lord led Chris and her husband to a developing community where He continues to use them and their family to impact the lives of their neighbors. Jesus commissioned His people to disciple every nation in His Name. Although you or I may never set foot on foreign soil in an official "missionary" capacity, we can reach the world – the world outside our windows.

In the crazy quilt of life,
I'm glad to have good friends in my block.

~ 35 ~
The Kitchen Woodbox
Submitted by Jane Doe of Anytown, USA

After being married a number of years, my husband and I finally had all our ducks in a row and decided we were ready to start our family. All the plans in place, I was certain the moment we discontinued our attempts at preventing it, we would be pregnant. But, it didn't work out that way.

Month after month my cycles continued, followed by years of infertility testing – ultimately revealing absolutely nothing. We prayed constantly throughout this frustrating time, but finally reached our breaking point. No more tests. No more procedures. No more failed attempts. We decided to adopt.

Reams of paperwork and thousands of dollars later, we completed our home study and obtained approval from the various institutions the government deemed necessary. Our church, family and friends prayed for us throughout the process – and for the baby who would be placed in our waiting arms.

Eighteen months into the adoption process we received a referral for a baby boy. Only two months later we traveled overseas and brought him home, our miracle baby. We rejoiced, along with everyone who prayed for us and with us.

John was sweet natured and an easy baby, with the exception of some mighty and long lasting temper tantrums. He was model beautiful, and the light of our lives.

By the time he reached third grade we began to notice he was falling behind both socially and academically. His teacher said we should expect more from him.

The following year John's fourth grade teacher suspected something was wrong, but didn't know what. In fifth grade we had him tested and were informed he had a rather serious case of ADD, affecting more than one part of his brain. We followed the doctor's advice and put him on medication. Things improved for a while.

Middle school revealed John's social deficits on a greater scale. By eighth grade his tantrums escalated to four-hour events provoking us to get him into counseling. We met with a psychologist. He evaluated our son and felt there was something wrong beyond ADD, but wasn't sure what it was. John improved under this psychologist's care, so we shook off the disconcerting feelings and prepared for high school.

High school had its ups – and some terrible downs. John never quite fit in; he had a small handful of friends, but he anguished over establishing relationships and becoming part of the crowd. He was taken advantage of, physically attacked, and emotionally raked over the coals. It broke our hearts to see the pain in his countenance.

The teachers all loved him, and he began to make some new friends his senior year. We continued praying and counseling, and we really thought things were looking up when he graduated from high school with honors.

College came, and everything seemed to be wonderful. John's grades were excellent, and he had finally established some tight friendships – or so we thought. His friends turned out to be con artists, convincing John to turn over his college bank account to them and worse. Following his psychologist's advice, we took our son for in-depth emotional, behavioral, physical, and psychological testing. The results came back that with John's symptoms, he could be the poster child for Asperger's Syndrome.

Asperger's is a form of autism, and after the diagnosis was made, we were stunned he hadn't been diagnosed earlier.

Many very successful people have Asperger's, but we are facing years and years of psychological and psychiatric counseling to get and keep John on track. He is a good five years behind socially, which is not uncommon for people with Asperger's. He may have a happy and successful life – but there's just no telling if, how or when things are going to turn out.

This story is still being written. The frustration, grief and cost involved in having a child with disabilities are at times overwhelming. We run the gambit of emotions constantly – worry, hope, anger, peace. We question how and why this beautiful child has so many problems when so many believers have been praying for him since before he was even conceived.

It doesn't make sense, and I don't know that it ever will. What I do know is that the Lord is there when I cry out – that He is with me when I doubt His love for me – and that in the blink of an eye everything will become clear. My hope for John's future rests in Christ, and when I remember that, the weight I carry is somehow lighter.

✼

I love walking into my kitchen and nuking my mug of coffee. I like my coffee hot. None of that cold coffee-a-chino stuff for me. Hot . . . piping hot! That's what I like.

Not so many generations ago, getting a hot cup of coffee required a lot more effort. I enjoy historical novels, and I've read about the time required felling trees, chopping firewood and keeping kitchen woodboxes filled with fuel for cooking and heating homes before other fuels were available.

Day after day, armloads of chunks and sticks and pieces of wood were carried in to kitchen woodboxes. To the one cutting and hauling, it seemed an unproductive task. The box always needed to be replenished. It was an unending cycle with no end in sight.

As I selected the name *The Kitchen Woodbox* for Jane's story (and no, that is not her real name, nor John her son's), I remembered a sermon I heard about the miracle of provision. It was about a widow woman and her son.

During a dire famine, a prophet asked a widow woman to make him something to eat. The woman had only enough oil

183

and meal to make one last cake for herself and her son to share before they both starved to death. Wisely, the widow offered to the Lord's servant what she had, and God sustained them all through the next three years.

At the end of those years, the three of them could have looked in the meal barrel and oil flask and said, "We're no further ahead than we were three years ago." But instead, they recognized the miracle of God's daily provision.

The days that Jane, you or I face the grind of "filling the woodbox" or making one more meal, or (fill in the blank), I pray the Lord reminds us that He is the source of everything we need – for today and tomorrow.

When things don't make sense, when the routine looks like it will never end, when we are clueless where our paths are leading or how our lives will turn out, let us remember Jane's admonition to look to the Lord, and He will lighten our loads.

~ 36 ~
Arkansas Traveler
Submitted by Pastor Paul Phillips of Floyd, Iowa

Ronnie McWilliams and I were born just three days apart. He came first on December 9, 1952, and I followed on December 12 – practically "womb mates" we often joked.

Our mothers shared the same hospital room after our births. We attended the same schools, went to the same church and played on the same basketball team. In May of 1971, we graduated from the same high school – an exciting year because our team, the White Hall Bulldogs, made it to the state basketball tournament.

After graduation, Ronnie attended the University of Arkansas at Little Rock. I enrolled at Arkansas State University in Jonesboro. Whenever possible we visited back and forth. During that time, we had a conversation that remains with me to this day. Ronnie seemed depressed, and I was going through an identity crisis of my own.

"You don't really believe there's a God that cares about us, do you?" Ronnie blurted out as we drove home from a night of partying.

"I believe in God. I believe He is the Creator and somehow directs our lives," I responded.

"I don't believe in a personal God," Ronnie insisted. "I think we were just born, and we're on our own, and we do the best we can with the cards we've been dealt."

One day during the spring of my sophomore year at Arkansas State, I returned to my dorm after class and plopped down on my bed. I was awake but relaxed when, as if I was dreaming, I saw myself standing in a park holding a Bible. There were 20 to 30 young people sitting on the ground cross-legged listening to me share about Jesus.

As I lay on the bed, a Presence enveloped me and the atmosphere in my room changed. I looked to see if anyone was there, but I was alone. This powerful Presence became stronger, and I realized I was not dreaming. I was wide awake, but couldn't comprehend what I was experiencing. The Presence permeated every part of my being. Overcome with emotion, I began to weep.

I jumped up from my bed, ran to the sink and splashed cold water on my face attempting to shock myself back to reality. The vision left, but the Presence lingered. I peered in the mirror and felt strongly directed to move back in with my parents right away. I knew deep within that I needed to make immediate, drastic changes in my life. Without hesitation, I packed my bags and returned home.

Physically moving from campus did nothing to abate my desire for the party lifestyle. When I arrived back home, I surrounded myself with the wrong kind of friends and continued making the same bad choices. One Sunday morning my father stuck his head in my room and asked, "Paul, are you going to church this morning?"

I had been sound asleep. Without opening my eyes I let out a groan and shook my head no.

"It's a fearful thing to fall into the hands of an angry God," my father warned.

My parents' rules cramped my walk on the wild side, so I rented an apartment with a couple of my buddies. I was only there a few months when I was arrested for marijuana possession. Facing my parents after my arrest was one of the most difficult things I have ever done. There were no heated verbal exchanges, but my mother let me know how disappointed she and my father were in my choices.

I started working at my father's business and enrolled at the University of Arkansas in Pine Bluff. One of our customers, an older gentleman named Mr. Reed, invited me to revival meetings at a local church. Still stinging from the results of my recent poor choices, I agreed to attend.

When I told my father about the revival, he said he would like to go with me. The first night I felt such a drawing to respond to Jesus. It was as if I was "homesick" for Him. The congregation sang the old hymns of the church, and a sweet Presence filled the sanctuary. I recognized that Presence – the same One who visited me in my dorm.

The next night my father and I again attended the special service. When the altar call was given, I felt such a pull to go forward and give my heart to Jesus. The Holy Spirit made it clear that I was at a crossroads. I knew if I continued down the path I was on I would live a life full of regret. Merciful Jesus offered me the opportunity to choose another path. I knew enough to realize that if I followed His ways, I would still face difficult days, but I also knew He would be with me on the journey. I went forward that night, repented of my sins and gave my heart to Jesus.

Soon after my life-changing experience, I surrendered to the call to preach. I knew I had to see Ronnie and tell him of my decision. I hoped and prayed he would have a spiritual encounter of his own.

"Ronnie!" I exclaimed, "I have found what we have been searching for."

"That's great, Paul! I've heard where people in the ministry can make a lot of money; especially if you play on people's emotions, like start an orphanage or feed hungry children."

Ronnie didn't "get it."

After I came to Christ I devoured the Word and surrounded myself with godly people. I also attended every church service I could. One night a missionary from Mexico spoke to my home Bible study group. When he concluded, we had a time of prayer during which the missionary walked directly to me and began to pray. He spoke these words over me: "The vision you had will come to pass in the next few days."

187

I was stunned. I remembered the "dreamlike" experience in my dorm room. Could that be the vision the missionary was talking about? But how would he know what I had seen? I'd never met this man, and I wasn't even sure if you called what I experienced a "vision." As I drove home from the meeting, so many questions filled my head. I pondered all the events of the day excitedly anticipating what God had planned.

The following morning my phone rang. It was my pastor.

"Paul, I would like you to give the devotions at the youth retreat this weekend up in the Ozark Mountains."

My mind raced to the previous night. Could this be the fulfillment of the vision God had given me?

Days later I stood before a group of young people, and I could barely believe my eyes. It was exactly as I had seen in the vision. Without a doubt I knew that Almighty God ordained this moment, and I knew that what I had experienced in my dorm room came from Him.

From time to time Ronnie and I saw each other, but it was apparent our lives were going in two totally different directions. I continued to love Ronnie through our differences. I knew that if he could just experience God's love for himself, it would change his life forever, but no matter how hard I tried, Ronnie let me know he was not interested.

The years marched on. I graduated from East Texas Bible College in Tyler, Texas, and became the pastor of a small church in rural northern Iowa. Early one morning the phone rang. It was my mother calling from Arkansas.

"Paul, Ronnie is dead."

A tidal wave of memories flooded over me as Mama continued, "He committed suicide."

I sat dazed. Scenes flashed before me. Past conversations with Ronnie replayed in my thoughts, and waves of grief swept over me. Ronnie and I began our journeys on the same path – a path that forked in two directions the day Jesus stepped into my dorm room.

I bowed my head to pray and wept for Ronnie's family. And I thanked God for revealing Himself to me.

✖

As I researched the quilt pattern *Arkansas Traveler,* I was amazed to find two completely different patterns with the same name. How fitting for Pastor Phillips' story of two men traveling on two different paths.

One of the *Arkansas Traveler* patterns is a star/pinwheel shape with blocks that connect in a visually pleasing, fluid design. The other features crazy intersections of fragments of triangles and rectangles, a haphazard scheme of non-connecting pieces that makes me rather dizzy when I look at it.

The application to this story takes little embellishment on my part, and I leave it to you to ponder. However, I will speak to another aspect of Pastor Phillip's story. The account of these two childhood friends encourages me to reach beyond the surface responses of those I come in contact with.

Ronnie rejected over and over the very answer to his unanswered questions. I credit Pastor Phillip's continued attempts to reach out to his friend in love. Every person ultimately makes their own decision, but regardless of the outward rejection of the good news of Jesus, the heart-longing for Him remains – even if unrecognized – or seemingly unwelcome.

Look beyond what you see. Keep planting. Keep watering. Keep walking beside the weary travelers with a hand out, a shoulder near, a heart open.

Chains do not hold a marriage together.
It is threads,
hundreds of tiny threads
which sew people together through the years.
~ Simone Signoret

~ 37 ~
Pig's Tail
Submitted by Maria Taormina of Grand Blanc, Michigan

I never knew my father's parents. Of pure Sicilian descent, my father was expected to marry a Sicilian, but he fell in love and married a French Canadian girl he met at a USO dance while serving in the Air Force. His decision angered his parents, and they had nothing further to do with him or his new wife.

The newlyweds settled in Hammond, Indiana, where they started their family – my family.

The highlight of every childhood summer was a month-long visit with my mom's parents. Our times with Grandma (Mimi) and Grandpa (Pipi) were all the more special since we lacked any connection with my dad's parents. When the wonderful day finally arrived, my parents loaded the car, and with much excitement we tumbled inside, trying to be patient as my father drove us all the way from the crossroads of America to the family farm in McGregor, Canada.

I loved the farm, especially the old house Pipi built stone by stone with his own hands. Royal blue shingles covered the two-story home and an ornate veranda shaded a large, brightly colored stained glass window in the living room. Pear trees lined the driveway that led into a large, circular yard. Across the driveway were the pump house and the chicken coop. Alongside these buildings was a huge shed full of farm equipment. At the back of the yard, a big red barn had a brown tiled silo attached with the words Alfred J. Martin and Sons painted in large letters across the top of the silo. It stood as a greeting to everyone who came in the driveway.

The 360-acre farm produced tomatoes, corn, wheat and oats; dairy cows provided milk for sale and the chickens provided eggs and hens which were also sold. Pipi, with the aid of only a second grade education, was a hard working, honest man who prided himself in his family and name. I could go into town and say, "I'm Alfred Martin's granddaughter," and that was as good as gold. I loved spending this time with Mimi and Pipi – and Uncle Phil and Aunt Lucille who lived next door with their eight children.

Pipi got up early every morning. After carrying in wood to fire the stove, he sat in his rocking chair in quiet contemplation and morning prayer. Sometimes the creaking of that old chair woke me and we would sit and talk.

The scent of cherry tobacco filled the air as Pipi rocked. He smoked his pipe with one hand and kept the other on the handle of a fly swatter that lay on the arm of his rocking chair. Some mornings, as I sat in a chair near him, he would tell tale after tale of "How the deer got his antlers" or "The devil that came to take Eva to the dance." Then Mimi would wake up and fix our breakfast, and the day on the farm would begin.

Everyone had a job on the farm. It was my responsibility, morning and night, to gather eggs from the chicken coop. Grasping the large metal pail, I quietly walked into the dimly lit wooden shed. A long wooden container that looked like shoe boxes sitting next to each other housed the nesting chickens inside. Walking slowly, so I would not disturb the chickens on the floor, I bolstered my courage and stuck my hand under the clucking, pecking hens to retrieve the eggs. It was a scene that would have made an nice feature in a scary movie. Relieved when I finished the job, I carried the pail to the house, careful not to break any eggs.

If Mimi needed apples, I picked them from the orchard – and strawberries from the berry patch. I took only what was needed and learned to waste nothing. At my grandmother's side I learned to can pickles, tomatoes and fruit as well as how to cook and sew.

Cows, pigs and chickens, my barnyard pets, became family dinners. I was sad to see them go, but after a day on the farm I was hungry for one of Mimi's delicious suppers. Everything tasted better there because it was made from scratch.

As I got older, Pipi let me pick tomatoes. It was long, hot backbreaking work, yet enjoyable times with my siblings and cousins. The occasional splash of a rotten tomato pitched by Uncle Phil was part of the fun.

When it was time to harvest the wheat, we younger ones were allowed to ride along. The men ran the machinery, and I held on to the back of the wagon as the wagon bed filled. I stood clinging to the rail, grain running through my toes, the warm sun shining on my face.

When the job was done, Uncle Phil sat on the edge of the wagon and caught grasshoppers in his hands. He pretended to throw them in his mouth and told me how much he loved to eat them, especially fried. He took great pleasure in taking a can of molasses (oil he told us), pouring it on two fingers, licking it off and proclaiming to his wide-eyed audience how delicious it was.

On Sundays, we attended church and heard Mass in French. The remainder of the Martin relatives, who comprised a large portion of the parishioners, greeted us there and made us feel welcome.

God was very much a part of my grandparents' everyday life, and they instilled in me the value of God in my life. It made me appreciate my family, develop a knowledge and love for gardening and wonder at God's purpose in it all. One day in particular I'll never forget. Mimi had a plastic barometer that sat on a shelf in the boot room of the house. It was a plastic house and depending on the weather the Dutch boy or girl would circle out of the doorway – a cheap novelty but an accurate weather indicator. This day, the boy and girl whirled violently in their little house.

"Mimi, why are they doing that?" I asked.

"It means bad weather is coming."

I glanced across the fields and saw black clouds had formed; thunder rolled and lightning crossed the sky. A funnel cloud off in the distance spouted a tornado that spun across the fields heading straight toward the farm.

"What do I do, Mimi?" I asked in a panic.

"Call all the children, run and lay them on the floor of the milk house," she shouted. The milk house was a small building next to the barn. When the children were safely tucked away, I ran back to the house to find Mimi hurriedly removing her clean underwear (pantaloons as we called them) from the clothesline. The winds were howling and the tornado spun closer and closer toward the farm. I clung to the line, attempting to help Mimi gather her pantaloons as they gyrated in the wind. She was determined her underwear would not end up in the yard of the old hermit whose farm was across the street.

I screamed at her to come with me to the milk house then watched in amazement as the tornado reached the edge of the farm, lifted back into the sky and touched down again on the other side of the property. It was a miracle, and I was grateful to God no one was injured – and Mimi was spared the embarrassment of having to retrieve her pantaloons from "Old Ed" the hermit.

Every New Year's Day, Mimi and Pipi hosted an open house. My dad drove through many a snowstorm so we could all be together for a feast of chicken, beef, vegetables, meat pies and desserts. We ate in shifts, with the younger cousins washing the dishes. It was a time to gather, catch up on the details of life, laugh and most importantly, to know you were accepted for yourself.

My relatives were not immune to arguments. Mimi and Pipi sometimes disagreed. They spoke their minds, and the next day it was over. On occasions when we children had quarrels, Mimi would say, "Even the pigs oink at each other every day in the barnyard." Family is family, and there was never an issue that could not be resolved and forgiven.

Mimi and Pipi are gone now, as are my parents and the rest of my aunts and uncles who so lovingly made up my memories of the farm. A bad windstorm knocked over the barn and silo that once stood so proudly bearing the name Alfred J. Martin and Sons.

Though the farm is not the working farm of many years ago, my cousin Jim lives there and grows soybeans and works a non-farming job. Another cousin, Dale, built his home on part of the acreage, and each Boxing Day he continues the open house tradition. Though not the feast of years gone by, Dale and his wife feed the hungry bellies and warm the hearts of those who remember the summer days shared decades ago with Mimi and Pipi.

Every September, many of the family gather for a reunion at a McGregor park. I am part of the older generation now, and it is important to me to spend time with the younger "Martins" of our family. I am the only one of my sisters who returns to Canada. They say it is not the same. Nothing ever is, but I want to stay connected. Our family, the farm and all the memories have helped shape who I am, and over the years I have learned that nothing is worth losing family bonds.

When children don't meet their parents' expectations – like my father disappointing his mom and dad (for valid reasons or not) – they're still family. When days are hot and long, and the rows of tomatoes that need picking seem endless, the companionship of a sister, cousin or a crazy Uncle Phil makes it worthwhile. As good as life gets, and as hard as life sometimes is, family is family, given to each other by the Lord. When my "barnyard" gets noisy with clucking and squallering, I reflect on the lessons I learned as I sat next to Pipi on those early mornings and remember Mimi's words, "Even the pigs oink at each other every day in the barnyard."

195

Family is family. No matter what.

I lived through several years without speaking to one of my close family members. I felt justified. Wronged. Righteous in severing the relationship.

Then why did it bother me so much? How come I, the one who walked away, was not at peace? Because God hard-wired families to belong to each other – regardless.

After those years of quiet unrest, I wrote to the one I felt wronged me seeking restoration. I wasn't even a Christian at the time; I just knew deep within me it was the right thing to do.

Decades have passed, and warm fuzzies did not immediately regenerate in my heart at the time of reconciliation, but the Lord has brought healing in the relationship. I actually like being with the person I once cut out of my life. And I'm thankful for that.

I really enjoyed Maria's story, and we shared a good laugh at the title, *Pig's Tail.* The next time you and your spouse are squabbling, or the kids (or your congregation) are making you crazy because they won't stop picking at each other, remember, "Even the pigs oink at each other." Regardless of the noise, they're still pigs . . . and they're still in the pigpen together . . . unless they've made a trip to the butcher, and I think the pigpen's a better place to be, even with a little oinking.

~ 38 ~
Buzzard's Roost
Submitted by Julie Arduini of Youngstown, Ohio

Precious Hannah filled my days with joy. After years of fighting infertility, I knew without a doubt my baby was a gift straight from Heaven. Following all the struggles to conceive, carry to full term and give birth, I was delighted by the arrival of my happy, healthy girl. The years of disappointment and loss faded in the sweet contentment of being Hannah's mommy.

Strong faith in God carried me through the trying years before Hannah's birth; however, when my little one turned two months old, my faith took a heavy blow. Diagnosed with congenital hypothyroidism, Hannah required immediate medical attention to combat possible developmental delays. Her health status changed from "well baby" to "at risk," and fear set in.

Unfortunately, an error occurred in the timing concerning the administration of her medications that made my husband and me wary the next time Hannah needed medical attention. A month later, during Thanksgiving week, Hannah contracted a cold. We were hesitant to return to the same doctor whose office erred in her previous treatment, but we had not established a relationship with a new pediatrician. After all, it was just a cold. What could possibly go wrong?

Reluctantly, we took Hannah to the doctor's office where after a cursory examination, her pediatrician prescribed Robitussin© with codeine. I was uneasy about giving such a strong medication to an infant and questioned the doctor. He assured me it was the best treatment for her condition – the stronger medication would deter her chances of getting croup. It was his belief every household should have this medication on hand.

I filled the prescription and gave the dosage indicated to Hannah, but her condition did not improve. Instead, as each hour passed, her symptoms became more severe and she weakened into a lethargic state. When I put her down for a nap, an overwhelming urgency compelled me to check on her. I rushed to her crib and found her completely gray, her pulse barely detectable.

It took a medical transport team from a pediatric intensive care unit two hours away to save Hannah's life. Her diagnosis was croup – complicated by doctor error. As gently as he could, the ICU doctor explained that Hannah should not have been given the medicine her pediatrician prescribed.

I fought the anger welling inside me. While my husband and I were two hours away from home in an ICU watching our baby fight for her life wrapped in tubes and connected to machines, our doctor was enjoying Thanksgiving dinner with his family.

On the brighter side, I was very thankful that after only a two-day stay, the hospital released Hannah declaring her a well child with no long-term concerns. A great diagnosis for my little girl, but my experience left me with a spiritual diagnosis that was not so optimistic. I was angry and paralyzed by fear, unable to leave my daughter for even a moment.

Images bombarded my mind. Pictures replayed in my thoughts Over and over I envisioned finding Hannah completely gray. I was obsessed with worry. What if she needed the transport team again? I was terrified the local emergency department would not know how to keep my baby alive. Many of the procedures performed at the local ER during the last episode had left Hannah scarred physically and me emotionally.

Each nap, every bedtime left me in absolute panic. Questions swirled around my mind unceasingly – *Is she breathing? Is she gray? It's been ten minutes, should someone check on her?*

I no longer trusted the monitor. My husband and I were in Hannah's room constantly, leaning on her to feel the rise and fall of her tiny chest. I was blinded by fear, afraid if I missed a moment of Hannah's breathing, she would die without me there to save her.

After months of prayer I finally realized the hold fear had gained on my life. The Lord used the memory of a Gaither Homecoming concert I attended six years earlier to help me get victory over my anxiety. I recalled during the concert Bill Gaither shared his experience after a heart procedure. The treatment went well, but afterwards left him anxious and scared about his future. He confessed his fears to fellow Homecoming singer Vestal Goodman, and with dramatic gestures Bill related Vestal's response.

One hand on a hip and the other one wagging in the air, she reminded Bill in no uncertain terms that he is the one who wrote *Because He Lives* – and that songs like that and lives like Bill's are about faith. Fear and faith never mix, Vestal exhorted, and she told Bill he had to choose one or the other. She ended her motherly rebuke with the hope that as the author of one of the most famous modern Christian songs, he "best be choosing faith." As I remembered the concert, I knew the Lord was prompting me to release my fear and telling me that I "best be choosing faith" for myself.

Bill Gaither would probably agree with me that it's a good thing God only asks for mustard seed-sized faith. Anything bigger I could not produce. I finally learned to "let go and let God." And Hannah is living proof of God's faithfulness. She has had a few asthmatic-type relapses since her hospitalization, but nothing that compares to the frightening experience at the pediatric ICU. Hannah's new pediatrician proclaimed her a "well child with a very bright future ahead of her." We also forgave the doctor, which truly set us free.

Nine months after Hannah's hospitalization my husband changed jobs and we moved out of town. The move gave us a new beginning in many ways. Like Bill Gaither's song says, we face unknown tomorrows, but God holds them all in His hands.

�֍

Julie's story, titled after the *Buzzard's Roost* quilt pattern, reminds me of the importance of trusting in God's hands what He has placed in ours.

None of us truly owns a person, a piece of property, a car, a job, or . . . you name it. The very breath in our lungs, the ability to lift hand to mouth, the mental capacity to string words together in coherent pattern – these are all gifts from God. The Lord gives into our lives, and everything ultimately belongs to Him.

In North America, most people think of buzzards as scavenging birds that feed on the carcases of dead animals – like vultures. Zoologists know this is incorrect species identification, but for our purposes, we'll go with our traditional understanding of the term.

When I think of buzzards, I think of an old western movie . . . a wounded cowboy sprawled out on the ground, thrown from his horse, stranded on the open range, parched, dry, no water in the canteen. He knows death is near when the buzzards start circling, and he weakly attempts to shoo them away with his dusty cowboy hat. Some old rough rider or Indian comes along and saves the day, and the buzzards lose their lunch.

As children of God, it's not our responsibility to shoo away the buzzards of fear circling overhead, nor give them a place to roost. When we give fear a foothold, it often "legs up" into the saddle and takes over the reigns, controlling our emotions and responses.

Our response is to trust God. Trust overcomes fear. Psalm 56:4 says "In God I trust; I will not be afraid." Did you see that semicolon there? That means those two phrases are linked together. When we really trust God, fear has no "roosting place."

~ 39 ~
Lone Star
Submitted by Carolyn McKenzie of Auburn Hills, Michigan

I walked into my mother's room and saw divorce papers on her dresser. That's how I discovered my parents were divorced.

I was 16 years old. To deal with the devastation and pain, I began abusing drugs, alcohol and cigarettes. And I mean *abuse.* I never just drank, I had to get vomiting, passed out drunk.

One night, while I sat watching a cigarette burn out in the dark, the Lord spoke these words to me, "If you stay on this path, you will die before you reach 30." That got my attention.

My grandmother invited me to a revival, and that night, I received the Holy Ghost speaking in fluent Chinese. My conversion and drastic life change put such a wide gulf between my mother and me that she did not speak to me for the next 15 years.

At 18 I married a young man in the church and soon became pregnant. Three months later I miscarried. Soon after that, my husband left me. I discovered he had been sexually involved with several women while we were married, including some of my close friends and family members.

Soon after my divorce, I lost my job and came down with pneumonia. I was in an accident that totaled my car. My father remarried, my old friends from before I got saved were gone. At church I was no longer part of the singles or the marrieds. I was completely disowned by my mother, my husband abandoned me and my baby was dead.

We are troubled on every side, yet not distressed; we are perplexed, but not in despair; persecuted, but not forsaken; cast down, but not destroyed. (2 Corinthians 4:8-9)

So now there I was, utterly and completely alone. Except for God. I was stripped of everything and everyone. It was just Jesus and me.

I wanted to die, but two things kept me from killing myself. One was my fear of hell, and the other was that I could not bear to hurt my father. I wanted so badly to crawl into the black box surrounding me, to turn the lock and never come out.

In prayer one day, I was pouring out all my pain and sorrows to the Lord, and for the second time in my life He spoke to me. Now at a time like this I would have expected Him to speak words of pity and comfort, but what He said actually startled me. Here's what he said, "You've taken long enough, it's time to start giving."

Mind you, I'd only been a Christian less than two years, and I felt I had nothing to give at the time. I didn't even fully understand what God meant, but I was sure He had spoken those words to me.

Right after that, my pastor's wife came up to me and asked me to start teaching Sunday school. That was my turning point. Instead of focusing on my pain and trouble, I began to focus on others and really study the Word of God.

Out of my utter aloneness, Jesus taught me that giving of myself to others was the means for me to receive my own healing and restoration.

The *Lone Star*, a favorite quilt pattern since the 1880s, is a difficult pattern to master. It begins with a single eight-pointed star fashioned in one color or pattern. Subsequent rows of varying colors and patterns radiate from the center motif. The star may be as small as three rows fashioned into blocks and pieced together, or the single star may continue to grow, layer after layer, until it covers an entire quilt top in a kaleidoscope effect.

Carolyn's difficult situation, so painful at the time, is now relegated to a foggy memory of a distant past. Happily married for over 30 years, the Lord blessed Carolyn with sons, daughters-in-law, and grandchildren who all join her and her husband on the pews of our church.

"You are the richest person I know," I told her at her grandson's dedication. The treasure the Lord bestowed upon her greatly outweighs any losses she experienced in her youth.

Carolyn's *Lone Star* status changed when she began investing herself in the lives of others. As my wise pastor's wife says, "When we take care of the things important to God, He takes care of the things important to us." And the Lord did that for my friend.

I'm so glad Carolyn did not crawl into her "black box" and give up. When I faced a crisis in my life, she devoted herself to seeing me and my family through the difficult time. I don't know what I would have done without her, and I appreciate the way she continually models God's love and compassion for others -- dispersing deeds of kindness and charity like the rippling rings of a *Lone Star* quilt.

A good friend
is like a warm quilt
wrapped around the heart.

~ 40 ~
# Hopes and Wishes
Lori Wagner

Two c-sections: one an emergency and one scheduled, but how I wanted to have this third baby the way God made them to come out. Believe me, I'm thankful for modern medicine. I would probably be dead without it. Still, the desire to deliver a child, instead of a child being cut from my womb, was what I was dreaming of.

My firstborn, Noelle, came the day after my Daddy died. I was already a week past my due date and hoped to make it to the funeral in another state. So my doctor agreed to induce me. After 20 hours flat on my back with a fetal monitor screwed into my baby's scalp tracking her heart rate, my labor failed to progress past two centimeters. I was contracting every minute, the intensity actually registering off the chart, and the baby's heart rate was in distress. So off we went to an operating room where my belly was cut open for the first time. I remember the weight of my organs being moved to clear the passage for the baby. It felt like a Mack© truck parked on my stomach.

Then I looked into the dark brown eyes of my slimy baby girl, and it was worth it all. She made eye contact with me and we stared at each other. She was just beautiful and so peaceful, too. And in one way, being in the hospital holding my newborn baby was easier than being at my Daddy's funeral. I held new life in my arms.

Noelle was four when Charles was born. My doctor left the decision to try a natural delivery or schedule a c-section up to me. I wanted to deliver naturally, but again, my due date passed, and my concern grew strong for the baby's health. I had been exposed to Hungarian measles during my pregnancy, and tested positive for the disease in my bloodstream. Five ultrasounds disclosed no problems, but there was a niggling in my spirit, and against my personal desire, I opted for the c-section.

The doctor opened me up, the Mack© truck parked on my chest again. Then a loud silence filled the room. An attendant whisked the baby away. I heard no crying. *Was it a boy or a girl? What's wrong with my baby?* Terrified, I waited to hear what was going on. After an hour-long minute or two, I heard the baby cry in a connecting room, and I started to breathe myself.

When I was sewn up and in the recovery room, the doctor patted me on the arm and said, "That was the best decision you ever made." My healthy son had aspirated meconium. If I had waited another week, he could have suffered severe breathing issues requiring the use of a ventilator – or worse. Although I had wanted to wait and try for a natural delivery, I was so thankful I listened to that inner prompting and scheduled the c-section. Besides, I looked great in the pictures. My hair was still curled!

Less than 2 years later, at 32 years of age, I became a single mother. Cancer took my husband's life and it was just me, my babies and Jesus . . . or so I thought.

I knew a lot of people didn't understand when I remarried, and in my head I really didn't either. I just knew in my heart that God gave me another loving husband. And that having another man love me did not take away from the love I had with my first husband. God made room in my heart for both, like when a second child comes along. I tell people, "Some people don't get one good husband, and I got two."

With my new husband came an eight-year-old daughter who had some major adjusting to do when I "took her seat" in the front of the car, among other issues. But over time, and after many bumps in the road, things smoothed out. Beyond the supernatural – God working in our hearts – something unexpected and wonderful happened that tied all the loose ends of our mixed up family together. A baby.

I never expected to have more children. When my first husband underwent cancer treatment, I knew my childbearing was over. Shows what I know!

When I found out I was expecting, I was surprised. Of course, I knew exactly when it happened, but it just didn't seem real.

My new doctor supported my desire to try for a natural delivery. For months I prayed, and my friends and family joined with me, that I would be able to deliver this baby.

My due date approached, and I showed no signs of effacing or dilating. I tried every home remedy I heard of to get things going myself: castor oil, walking (even behind the lawn mower to the shock of those who saw my expanded frame waddling behind the self-propelled machine), and some I don't want to mention here in case my kids read this chapter.

I was out pruning in my front yard when the first contraction hit. I'd never gone into labor without the aid of inducing drugs. I smiled, rubbed my huge belly and continued working in the yard until I was sure. Soon, I was sure.

I told my husband, we ran the kids to my in-laws, and headed for the hospital. After checking in, a short time passed and, instead of the contractions getting stronger, they grew fainter and further apart. I was in tears. "But I wanted to have this baby naturally," I cried to my husband. "We've been praying for months," I said out loud, and to myself, *What good is praying anyway? God must not be listening or just doesn't care.*

I know. You're shocked. But that's what it felt like at the time.

Doctor Smith, a competent and patient man, understood my frustration. We had discussed many times how I wanted to go natural, and he said he would work with me. When my labor slowed, and I was told I should come back later, Dr. Smith saw my distress and suggested I try a topical gel to get things going. I was unwilling to use Pitocin© again, because of the nightmare contractions I had with the first baby, but I tried the gel, and it worked!

My contractions started again. And then I was wondering if I'd made the right decision, because they were really hurting. I mean, I knew labor was supposed to hurt, but wow, the vise clamping down in my uterus surpassed what I expected.

I received an epidural. It was the strangest thing. It took on one side of my stomach, eliminating the distress of the contractions, but on the other side, they were still going full force. The anesthesiologist shifted me around and tried to get the medicine flowing, but it never reached the full span of my uterus.

After a time, I decided perhaps I made a mistake and should have scheduled the c-section after all. What was I thinking when I said I wanted to go natural? Oh, Doctor Smith . . . I told him I changed my mind. Just get that baby out.

But the good doctor was used to working with frantic, laboring women. He reminded me how much I wanted to do this and that he had committed to help me. So we pressed on, well, I was the one doing the pressing, actually. And at 10:00 p.m. on the nose, a beautiful baby girl slipped into the world. I looked down at her wet, pink body still attached to mine in utter amazement. First, because my son was a girl . . . where were those missing parts I was expecting? Second, because God blessed me to deliver her.

I had been expecting a son. Not that the ultrasound said so – I just knew it. (See a pattern here about how much I really know?) I could tell from the way I carried the baby – like with Charles, not Noelle. Throughout the pregnancy, Bill and I spent 98 percent of our name-choosing time on boy names because I was so certain. Only three weeks before the delivery we decided, on the off chance the baby might not be a boy, we better pick a girl name. We made our lists and checked them more than twice, not agreeing on our choices. Then one day it clicked.

Bill had gone through an unwanted divorce. He would tell you himself he cried himself to sleep every night for a year. But, while marriage takes two, divorce only takes one, and the situation was out of his control.

I lost a husband to death. My babies lost their daddy. We had all the lemons we needed for gallon upon gallon of life's lemonade. Through our situations, the God of restoration and hope brought us together and gave us a new life, for ourselves, and in this new baby. We named her Hope.

�֍

Sometimes life doesn't bring us what we expect . . . certainly not what we signed up for. I recall at a conference I attended, the Lord spoke to my heart saying "Just because your life isn't what you expected, doesn't mean it can't be good." I remembered the Scripture that says, "He does all things well," and submitted my spirit to His Sovereignty . . . again. When my hopes and wishes don't line up with the Lord's, I would do well to remember the His words.

And sometimes – oh, those special sometimes – we get to stand on a mountain top and look down over the valleys and difficult passages it took to get there with joy. When my Hopey girl came, my feet were in stirrups, but my spirit was standing on a mountain top.

As you reflect on this story bearing the name of the quilt pattern *Hopes and Wishes*, you might have recalled some hopes and wishes of your own. I pray that many of them brought you joy, and for those that didn't work out the way you anticipated, remember that God does all things well. And when life doesn't work out the way you expected, it can still be good!

✣

Take your needle, my child,
and work at your pattern;
it will come out a rose by and by.
Life is like that –
one stitch at a time
taken patiently,
and the pattern will come out all right . . .
~ Oliver Wendell Holmes

~ 41 ~
The Backing
Lori Wagner

Cancer. At first we thought it was a temporary problem, perhaps a herniated disc. My husband had been playing "Mr. Fix-it" under a kitchen sink, and he was experiencing pain in his lower back.

The unexpected collapse of his spinal column occurred one evening when he was alone with our two children. Charles was still in diapers, only ten months old. Pete reached into the baby's crib to lift him out and fell to the ground with the baby in his arms. Charles was unharmed, but our lives were never the same again.

Pete was in agonizing pain and couldn't get off the floor. My five-year-old Noelle saw to the baby and attended her daddy as well as a five-year-old could. This was before we had cell phones, and it was hours before I returned from my meeting to discover what had happened to my family.

Pete was like most men. He thought he'd just "tough it out." There was no reason to go to the doctor . . . right? This pain would go away, and he'd get better on his own. Bodies heal themselves. God made them that way.

Sometimes, but not so for Pete. It took three weeks before I could convince him to go to the doctor. During that time, he was on the floor. I dragged a mattress in the living room for him to lie on because he couldn't stand or even make it to the bathroom. The world turned upside down.

Tenacious Pete. That he was. It was the reason he'd been so successful in his career designing automotive interiors for General

Motors, but it wasn't helping this situation. He said he wouldn't eat because he didn't want to have to go to the bathroom, but the days wore on.

Finally I convinced him to at least go to the chiropractor. He was in such pain it took a half an hour and all the tenacity he could muster to get from the house to the car only a few feet away.

X-rays indicated spinal degeneration. We didn't know exactly what that meant, but it didn't sound good.

Upon receiving the diagnosis, Pete opted for a program of physical therapy treatment. A visiting nurse came to our home for a preliminary evaluation. Part of the enrollment included a blood sample, which resulted in a call early the next morning advising us to proceed immediately to the hospital. There was something seriously wrong with his blood count and platelets.

The diagnosis was made: cancer. The prognosis was harsh: two weeks.

I'm so thankful God intervened and gave us an entire year. Many challenges presented themselves throughout that time. Physical, emotional, financial and spiritual roller coaster rides ensued. But God saw us through every step of the way.

In the beginning, just four days prior to the spinal collapse, God gave me a vivid dream that woke me from a sound sleep in the middle of the night. I sat up in bed startled and shaken as I remembered the details.

Pete and I were traveling up a steep mountain on a one-way road. It was an abstract, treacherous thing with no side rails, and along the way Pete began having pain. It increased to the point that I switched places with him while we continued driving upwards. There was no place to stop or turn around, so I drove on as his pain increased.

Oh, God, you have to get us off this mountain, I prayed, then I saw a wall of greenery in front of me. There was no way to know what was on the other side, but the Lord wanted me to trust Him and drive through it. There was no cliff. There was no boulder. It was the pathway down the mountain, and I took it safely to the bottom where I stopped the van and breathed a deep sigh of relief.

But as the tension released and my heart rate slowed, I looked to the passenger seat to see my Petey was gone. God had seen me safely down the mountain, but my husband was no longer with me.

Through the dream, the Lord prepared me for what was to come, then He faithfully walked beside us on our journey. All the way He told me to trust Him.

As the pieces of my life swirled about me, not knowing where they would land, I learned to trust God in a newer dimension. It was like living in the eye of a hurricane: a place of calm in the midst of a devastating storm.

Pete was "inpatient" for over 100 days that year, and the drive to the hospital took almost an hour. As I drove back and forth, the Lord gave me a song to sing that prepared me on the way there and kept me on the return trip home.

There is peace in the middle of the storm
Though the wind blows hard and long
In the dark of the night
Your Word's my guiding light
And I'll have peace in the middle of my storm

You know it's a divine strength that sustains you when you walk through this kind of valley. I never imagined being a widow at 32 with 2 small children to care for on my own, but through it all, I "laid my head upon His chest," and the Lord sustained me.

At the funeral, the choir sang "Trust in the Lord with all of thine heart, and lean not to thine own understanding, but in all thy ways acknowledge Him, and He shall direct thy path." The choir director selected the song. I had not requested anything in particular, and it was the perfect choice. My trust in God saw me through that difficult year, and continued to do so in the days to come.

�֍

The backing of a quilt is solid. It doesn't change. It's not pieced together, but strong. The backing of our life's quilt is our foundational trust in God. No matter what the top design looks like, it's the backing, our trust in God, that gives stability and strength.

As you face the unique challenges of your life, place your trust in God's hands. There is no safer place, and He can keep your heart at peace even as the storms of life swirl about you.

~42~
The Common Thread
Lori Wagner

The construction of a quilt requires many different materials and supplies, but one staple item is a must from the first stitch to the last. What keeps the patches patched and the binding bound? What secures backing and batting? Prevents shifting and bunching? What one element interacts with every facet of the coverlet?

A simple thread – a fine cotton filament unites every part – seen and unseen.

At the beginning of the process, the strand of thread slips easily through thin patches of fabric sewing them together into pleasing patterns.

When the piecing is complete, the thread takes on a new role as it bastes together three completely different components: the quilt top, a layer of batting and the backing. All this before the actual quilting begins.

Next – through all the layers basted together – lengths of thread meticulously, rhythmically journey up and down, in and out in swirling and linear choreography while little dips and puffs pirouette around the uniform stitches.

And finally, as the end of the crafting nears, double-fold binding encases the edges wrapping the full thickness of all the layers. The thread, laboriously pushed through all the layers with the aid of a sharp needle and thimble, continues its work until the quilt is complete, and then its journey ends.

215

Like the thread, the common factor throughout the quilt-making process, the Lord has given His people one incredible Scripture that unites every aspect of our lives. Not always easy to embrace or even understand, Romans 8:28 connects every situation and experience with a great promise – one that won't unravel in the difficult days.

And we know that all things work together for good to them that love God, to them who are the called according to His purpose. (Romans 8:28)

Individual experiences can overwhelm: the highs and the lows, the joys and the sorrows, the routines of everyday life. But when we take a moment to step back and take our eyes off the individual "quilt pieces," the situations we face, we gain a fuller, more discerning perspective. Truly, God's ways are higher than our ways, His thoughts higher than ours (Isaiah 55:9).

We rejoice in the good times – seasons of sunshine and gladness. We plow through the furrows of unremarkable workdays, plodding in row after row of habitual ritual, and vapid conversation as we face our jobs, our chores, and the same people doing the same things day after day after day. We suffer loss and cry tears of frustration and anger when life's difficulties don't make any sense to us. Just why does God allow children to become ill with terminal diseases? Does God devise life's tragedies and accidents? Tsunamis and hurricanes? Famine and pestilence?

Only God can truly answer these staggering questions. *Quilting Patches of Life* is not a theological study on such a difficult subject, but was written to share experience, build faith and impart hope.

We do know the Lord created a perfect world, and even in that utopian environment, sin entered. And now in our fallen world, we should not be surprised when we face challenging situations.

One thing is certain, my friend; God can and does give us the grace and strength we need to face each day. His grace is sufficient to live through and with the circumstances that weave in and out of our lives. And although things aren't always the way we would like, they can still be good. Because God is good. And He has good plans for His people.

For I know the plans I have for you declares the Lord, plans to prosper you and not to harm you to give you hope and a future. (Jeremiah 29:11 NIV)

Throughout the progressing developmental stages of our lives, we often encounter greater pressure and resistance along the path to spiritual maturity. In a physical quilt, strands of thread are cut, sewn and knotted throughout the entire process, but as the stages of production unfold, the actual needlework becomes more difficult.

As we mature in our walk with God, the pressure often seems greater as the Lord probes through deeper and thicker layers of our humanity – our very thought processes and innermost beings pierced by the Sword of the Word (see Hebrews 4:12). The thread, however, is constant – the thread of God's sovereign intention working throughout the fabric of our lives one stitch at a time. The Most High God connects and intertwines our days and circumstances into Master pieces of His creation.

Whether mountains or valleys
Or treadmills unending
A pattern of days
God's crafting, or mending

His purpose in focus
Our hearts safely rest
Believing, trusting
The Quilter knows best

Bits of bright joy
Dark segments of strife
The routine of existence
Patches of life

Affirming Faith Writing Contest Winners

Evans Bissonette *(King's Highway)* is a *storyteller* from a young age (a trait that often earned him time outs). Evans retired from a career in I/T to trade writing programs, documentation, and client manuals, for writing health and fitness, historical fiction, and children's books. His post-retirement articles have appeared in *Senior Living News*. Evans earned a B.A. from the Northwood University of Michigan-Midland. He and his wife Sue live in Troy, Michigan. They are the proud parents of three adult children, Jenna, Stacy, and Brad.

Brad Erlandson *(Job's Tears)* earned a B.A. in Theology from Toccoa Falls College and a Masters in Religion from Liberty University. He is the author of *Walking This Walk* published by Xulon Press. He speaks in churches on the subject of God's will in suffering and also speaks on behalf of Mothers Against Drunk Driving (MADD) at local public facilities.

Alan Hahn *(Rainbow Cactus)* earned a B.A. from the University of Michigan-Dearborn. His articles on parenting have been published in *Metro Parent Magazine*, and his business and marketing writing has been featured in *Detroit Chamber* publications and *Michigan Lawyers Weekly*. Alan and his wife Shawn live in Waterford, Michigan. They are the proud parents of two adult children, Brandon and Brittnie.

Melissa May Hoffmann *(Rose of Sharon)* is a registered nurse and lives in Rochester Hills, Michigan, with her husband Chris and children Anneliese and Benjamin. She writes mostly for pleasure, and this is her first published story.

Florence Koski *(Hens and Chicks)* lives in Covington, Kentucky.

Eileen Kruper *(Mariner's Compass)* lives in Troy, Michigan with her husband Gil. They're children, adopted in the 1980s, were born in South Korea.

Rachel Lowrence *(Crown of Thorns)* lives in Southfield, MI She is homeschooled, and a junior in highschool. She is an aspiring writer and also enjoys playing tennis, piano, and doing a wide range of crafts.

Maria Taormina *(Pig's Tail)* resides in Grand Blanc, Michigan, where her primary task since 1994 has been caregiver to her husband who sustained multiple injuries when he was electrocuted on his job. She is currently writing a book about his accident, caregiving and finding her own purpose – and simultaneously working on a children's poetry book. Maria and her husband raised two great children, Larry and Barbara. Maria's passion is writing. She loves to greet each sunrise with a cup of coffee and a chat with God thanking Him for her many blessings.

Sharon K. Wilson *(Pinwheel)* resides in Clarkston, Michigan, where she writes short stories for family and friends. She is currently involved in writing and reading for a grief support group and hospice care program.

John Wood *(Capital T)* lives in Las Vegas, Nevada.

FaithWriters
www.faithwriters.com

Julie Arduini *(Buzzard's Roost)* is a graduate of the Jerry B. Jenkins Christian Writers Guild (CWG) under the direction of Stephen and Janet Bly. She is the co-facilitator of the CWG Forum's "Missing Pages Book Club" and a contributing writer for the forum's blog. She also maintains her own blog and is a member of FaithWriters.
http://thesurrenderedscribe.blogspot.com

Karen Elengikal *(Beggar's Block)* is an inspirational author whose first book *Kidz Battle Zone* was released July 2007. Karen lives in Sydney, Australia, with her husband and six sons. Two driving passions compel Karen: developing and imparting to her children a deep, intimate relationship with Jesus, and capturing the incredible beauty and intricacies of God's creative genius through photography.
www.kidzbattlezone.com, www.Godinspired-PhotoArt.com

Julianne Jones *(Follow the Leader)* is an Australian writer currently living in New Zealand. A wife, mother of five, grandmother to one, and early childhood teacher, Julianne enjoys writing short stories, dramas, and inspirational articles. She is presently working on a young adult novel.

Carolyn M. Kenney *(Sunbonnet Sue)* has written weekly articles for her church bulletin for over four years, many of which were featured in a devotional book titled *Meditations of the Heart* published December 2003 by Author House. www.myspace.com/carolyn8390

Lissa M. Lee *(Whirlwind)* is a Louisiana resident. She works full time for a design firm and spends the majority of her free time pursuing her passion – writing. Published numerous times she still focuses on her original writing goal: "to bring clarity through creative communications."

Brad Paulson *(Britches)* is a construction superintendent by day and a freelance writer by night. He resides in Spokane, Washington, with his lovely wife Mardi and two sons, Will and Rob. He is a regular contributor to FaithWriters and a number of his short stories have been published in their anthology books. His work has also appeared in a variety of online Christian e-zines and websites.

Dixie Phillips *(Dove in the Window)* has been married to the love of her life, Paul, for 30 years. They have four grown children – Rachel, John, Beka and Libby. In her spare time, Dixie enjoys ghostwriting. Her work has been published by Abingdon Press, Standard Publishing, Elderidge Publishing, LIVE Publications and Guardian Angel Publishing. www.floydlighthouse.com

Paul Phillips *(Arkansas Traveler)* and his wife, Dixie, have served the congregation of the Gospel Lighthouse Church and Lighthouse Academy in Floyd, Iowa, for the past 26 years. His favorite pastime is fishing in Arkansas with his three brothers – Bill, Dennis and Don. www.floydlighthouse.com

Jan Ross *(Treasure Chest)* and her husband Ron make their home in Willard, Ohio. They are the parents of six wonderful adult children who have blessed them with twelve incredible grandchildren. As a missionary and president of Heart of God International Ministries, Jan's servant heart and deep passion to teach the Word of God continue to bear much fruit to the glory of God through her writing and global ministry outreach. www.heartofgodinternational.com

Irvin L. Rozier *(Joy Bells)* is the author of *My Walk with the Lord*, published by Selah Publishing Group, as well as various articles and poems available by searching online. Irvin retired from the U. S. Army and serves as chaplain for his local American Legion Post. www.selahbooks.com

Sandra Snider *(Garden Gate)* earned a degree in journalism and has worked as a freelance writer for the last 30 years. Sandra writes regularly for WebWomen Connect, and is widely published in books, newspapers, magazines, and on the internet. Sandra and her husband have one daughter and live in Minneapolis, Minnesota. www.nhlc.org.

David Story *(Brave Sunflower)* is a member of FaithWriters, where he has been a consistent entrant in the Writing Challenge and has had three of his entries place in the top ten. David has also published an e-book, titled, "Whispers." He and his family currently reside in Texas, where David is now working on his second novel, "The Prayer Chain."

Friends and Family

Cristina Broomfield, MA *(Evening Star)* is a Limited Licensed Psychologist and co-owner of Perspectives of Troy Counseling Center in Troy, Michigan. She co-hosts "Family Life Perspectives" on WMUZ 103.5FM in the Detroit area and is an adjunct faculty member of Rochester College. Cristina and her husband have five grown daughters and are grandparents to ten.
www.perspectivesoftroy.com

Patty Cayten *(Flower Basket)* joyfully abides in Niles, Ohio, with her incredibly handsome husband Michael and their six flowers from Heaven (although at times she calls them all stinkweeds). She has had many articles published on her fridge, and in her husband's lunchbox.

Randa Chance *(Turkey Tracks)* lives in San Antonio, Texas. She simultaneously wears the hats of mommy, preacher's wife, singer and speaker, and frequently tap dances when no one is watching. She finds strength in laughter and loves to walk in the snow.
www.thehopecenterchurch.org

Lisa Crump (Hole *in the Barn Door)* serves as National Coordinator Manager for the National Day of Prayer (NDP) Task Force where her responsibilities include publishing *Power Lines,* a newsletter for NDP volunteers. She lives in Colorado Springs with her husband Mickey.
www.ndptf.org

Christine Gibson *(Cathedral Window)* is a full-time wife to the world's most optimistic visionary and mom to their five children. Her interests include medicinal herbs and reading historical fiction. She illustrates children's publications and has written for and served as editor for *Moms, Inc., Newsletter* for three years.

Jeanne Grief *(Honeycomb)* is the mother of four girls, and grandmother of eleven. She spent most of her adult life as a professional seamstress. The last nine years of her "work" she owned and managed a Christian bookstore and gift shop from which she retired in December 2006. Jeanne is very active in various ministries at her church. She now enjoys more time with her husband David, children and grandchildren, travel, needlework, and of course, having a heart to heart with God several times a day.

Ann Kalajian *(Hosanna)* is the mother of three sons and grandmother to six. She was raised in Damascus, Syria, and moved to the United States in 1947, where she met and married Charles Kalajian. They were blessed with 49 years together. Ann lives in Manomet, Massachusetts, and her favorite pastimes (to the pleasure of her neighbors) are gardening and caring for her koi in her backyard pond.

Steve Lockman *(Dancing Bear)* graduated from the University of Minnesota with a BS in Social Work. He also earned a paralegal degree and Associate of Arts in general studies. Steve has served his community as a liaison for the disabled, as a church trustee and also in public office. He founded and runs Lockman Publishing Company, which provides ghostwriting, songwriting, marketing and advertising services.
www.thebookwriter.com

Bernie Lutchman *(Blind Man's Fancy)* is the author of *Two Minute Warning - Handbook of Effective Christianity for the 4th Quarter of Life* published by Xulon Press. He is a National Day of Prayer Coordinator for Springfield, Illinois, and the Communications Director of Business Men In Christ.
www.bernielutchman.blogspot.com

Carolyn McKenzie *(Lone Star)* is the mother of two grown sons and grandmother to Alexandra, Wesley and Blake. She also cared for seven children in the foster care system. Carolyn speaks at seminars on child/parent training and helping children with learning problems. She and her husband Craig live in Auburn Hills, Michigan.
www.childthrive.blogspot.com

Larry Patton *(Broken Dishes)* has been affected by cerebral palsy since birth, resulting in limited physical abilities. Despite many obstacles, he graduated from Wayne State University, worked for IBM for 16 years, and then founded Hurdling Handicaps Speaking Ministries as a means to encourage others to overcome life's obstacles with the help of the Lord. He is a member of the National Speaker's Association and has authored two books, *More Than An Average Guy* and *If He Can Do It, I Can Do It.* Larry lives in Troy, Michigan, with his wife Jenny and their two children Will and Anna.
www.hurdlinghandicaps.org.

Lisa Riley *(Black-Eyed Susan)* loves living in Berkley, Michigan, with her husband Mark. She is the mother of three gifts from God: Shannon, Joel and Rachel, and "Bubbie" to Hunter and Jackson. Lisa has a passion for young people and has taught Sunday school for over two decades.

Margie Stoller *(Garden Walk)* lives in Bloomfield Hills, Michigan. She and her husband have two adult children who they adopted from Korea as infants. They lived in Indiana, Minnesota and Colorado before moving to Michigan. Margie and John are enjoying John's semi-retired status and traveling whenever they can.

Suzanne Stoltz *(East to Eden)* works with Bott Radio Network as the Mid-Missouri Area Manager. Through previous positions at University of Missouri-Rolla, she worked with the *International Friends Program* and helped introduce the *No Apologies* abstinence program to the top educators in China. Sue oversees the Midwest Region for the National Day of Prayer. She and her husband Bob have been married 39 years and have three children and two grandsons.

Karrie Vandewater *(Anvil)* has a passion for ministering to the hurting. She has conducted weekly church services for women in a Michigan jail, and for boys incarcerated for drug-related crimes in a psychiatric hospital. She has also ministered to the elderly in nursing homes and assisted living centers. Karrie works with the Reclaim Kids program reaching out to AIDS orphans in Africa. Carrying a burden for the people of Germany, Karrie, her husband Greg and daughter Sara moved to Stuttgart, Germany, in 2005.
www.reclaimkids.org

Would you like your story considered for publication in
Quilting Patches of Life Vol. II?

E-mail your story to:
loriwagner@affirmingfaith.com

NOTES

The American Quilter's Society
P.O. Box 3290 Paducah, KY 42002-3290 USA
270.898.7903
www.AmericanQuilter.com

QuiltBus, the quilt store that comes right to your door.
www.quiltbus.com

FaithWriters, an encouraging community of Christian writers
learning and growing in a safe, caring environment.
www.faithwriters.com

Bibles Referenced (beyond KJV):
Holy Bible, New International Version (NIV) copyright© 1973,
1978, and 1984 by the International Bible Society.

Holy Bible, New King James Version (NKJV) copyright©1982
by Thomas Nelson Publishers.

The Bill Wagner Family
November 2005

For information on bulk orders of *Quilting Patches of Life,* or to schedule Lori Wagner for a speaking engagement, contact:

Affirming Faith
1181 Whispering Knoll Lane, Rochester Hills, MI 48306
(248) 909-5735
loriwagner@affirmingfaith.com
www.affirmingfaith.com

Also available:
Gates & Fences: Straight Talk in a Crooked World
Gates & Fences, now in its third printing, is highly recommended by pastors and youth leaders. In workbook format, this straight talking book uses humor, personal stories and solid teaching as it encourages youths and singles to consider the blessings of Biblical boundaries.

Soon to be released:
Gateway to the Sun
Gateway to the Sun is historical fiction, a chapter book for middle school+ readers as told by 13-year-old Huallpa, a Quechua Indian boy living under Inca rule in the Andes Mountains during the time of the Spanish conquest. An entertaining and educational book for all ages.